100 Years
of the
Snaefell Mountain
Railway

by
Stan Basnett
and
Keith Pearson

*L*eading *E*dge™
press and publishing

Published by Leading Edge Press & Publishing Ltd,
The Old Chapel, Burtersett, Hawes, North Yorkshire, DL8 3PB.
☎ 01969 667566

A CIP Catalogue record for this book is available from the British
Library.

ISBN 0 948135 59 X

Series Editor Stan Abbott
Designed by Hayley Beck
Sketch maps by Stan Basnett
Colour reprographics by Impression, Leeds
Printed and bound in Great Britain by Ebenezer Baylis & Son Ltd,
Worcester

---

*Title page illustration: Brand new Snaefell trackage at Lhergy Veg, 1895. The
wall was substantially buttressed in 1906. (Mather & Platt.) Note: Mather
and Platt (Machinery) Ltd is now part of Weir Pumps Ltd.*

Foreword

The 1993 centenary of the remarkable Manx Electric Railway was very much a milestone for us all at Isle of Man Railways.

It provided us with a marvellous platform to demonstrate to the world just how important our vintage railway system is, particularly at a time when people everywhere are increasingly interested by their heritage.

The events that we organised for the centenary helped to attract many people to the Island from the British Isles and much further afield, throughout the world, to see for themselves this working example of the "cutting edge" of Victorian engineering.

The success of the 1993 events gave us great encouragement as we considered the approach of the 1995 centenary of the Snaefell Mountain Railway.

Although complementing the Manx Electric Railway, the SMR is a separate running system, no less pioneering in its own right than the more extensive Manx Electric.

The construction of the line was not only accomplished in the remarkably short period of seven months, but it also provided an opportunity for the use of the revolutionary Fell system of braking using a central rail.

Although the original Fell system has been supplemented by a more modern form of braking, the railway remains, in essence, that which was built 100 years ago and to travel on the SMR today is to relive one of the great joys of the Victorian and Edwardian visitor to the holiday island of Mann.

I am once again pleased to endorse a Leading Edge RailTrail publication, aimed at encouraging visitors to the Island to combine the pleasures of walking the fells and glens with a ride on our railways. With its companion volumes, *The Isle of Man by Tram, Train and Foot* and *Hidden Places of Mann*, this book provides an ideal route by which to explore our rich heritage, encompassing not only railways and industrial archaeology, but also a fascinating ancient history that predates the arrival of Christianity.

I hope that it helps readers to enjoy their stay on the Island and will encourage them to return in the future. You will be made most welcome!

Robert Smith
Transport Executive, Isle of Man Transport
June 1995

Dedication

To the late Harold Gilmore
MER General Manager
1968-77
...and genial MER host to successive
generations of enthusiast visitors

Harold Gilmore. (W J Wyse)

Acknowledgements

On page 156 of *One Hundred Years of the Manx Electric Railway(1993)* appear substantial acknowledgements of help received from a wide ranging body of individuals, which continue valid here.

The core of the present text has its foundations in the Snaefell account in the earlier book, itself having origins in a 1955 publication. It is pleasant to record the continued support of members of the Fell family, and of my cartographer, John Cooke — and of John H Price, who has carefully maintained his own Snaefell record year by year.

It happened that the composition of this text coincided with a domestic relocation, and only help from the following has made possible what would otherwise (it sometimes seemed) be impossible!

Messrs Paul Abell, Stanley Basnett, Roger Sims (Librarian Archivist, Manx National Heritage), Captain Stephen Carter, Morris Faragher, Colin Goldsmith, George Lawson, Graham Warhurst and Dr Paul E Waters.

Contents

The Snaefell Story 1895 — 1995

This book partly represents an adaptation of the account given in Keith Pearson's *One Hundred Years of the Manx Electric Railway* (1993). The update, however, includes an account of the exciting programme currently (February 1995) in hand in connection with the celebrations planned for August of that year and some wider references to the Fell railways, both Manx and overseas.

The "Fell line" — a centre-rail adhesion mountain railway — was patented by John Barraclough Fell (1815-1902). The story of the Fell family and Fell Mountain Railways is the subject of Keith Pearson's impending book, as announced on page 64.

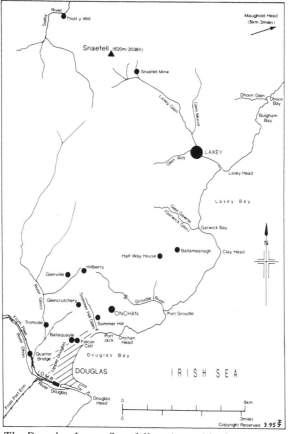

The Douglas-Laxey-Snaefell region, with place names appearing in Chapter 1 (John C Cooke)

Local Railway Geography, 1874-95

The Isle of Man's history as a 19th century resort has several distinct phases. In the 1870s it was essentially the preserve of the well-to-do, when whole families migrated to summer residences, accompanied by mountains of baggage and often their household servants. This was the era when the core of Island rail transport was established by the construction of the Isle of Man and Manx Northern steam railways. It left a substantial area minus any railway. By the 1880s this territory (extending up the east coast between Douglas and Ramsey, and by implication to Snaefell) had attracted the attention of entrepreneurs, who saw the possibility of earning a satisfactory return on a line northwards from Douglas. There was a potential for tourist traffic and for minerals — for at this date Laxey was an important mining centre (its small harbour already functioned in this export connection).

The relevant documentation which survives in the Manx Museum is a discontinuous one, although some of the surviving papers are almost intimately detailed. The known main groupings are two in number, and specifically from one of these springs today's Snaefell Railway (indeed, its route is almost certainly that which was first considered for a steam worked Fell line in 1887-8, or even two years earlier).

Outside this central element should be mentioned an earlier approach when William Lewis addressed a letter (dated January 1874) to banker G W Dumbell, in which he proposed a railway branching off the Douglas-Peel line (opened 1873) following the River Glass to below Glenville, then up a side valley to Hillberry and down the southern side of the valley of the Groudle River to Port Groudle. As this could only have served agricultural users and enjoyed a small volume of tourist traffic its lack of subsequent documentation is hardly surprising.

By the early 1880s one active Manx civil engineering professional had established himself on a wider stage. This was Daniel Cregeen (1821-1894) who was employed by H M Commissioners of Works in London and had designed a series of Island projects. One such example was a pedestrian tunnel passing under Douglas harbour, and by the 1890s he became enmeshed in a far more grandiose scheme for bridging the harbour.[1]

At this point it is assumed that Cregeen was, at the outset, the un-named engineer of the Douglas, Laxey and Ramsey Railway Company, which made a first public appearance on March 1, 1882 with a proposed capital of £130,000 in £5 shares. Of eight initial subscribers, three were

---

[1] *These topics are dealt with by Keith Pearson in the Journal of the Manx Museum, issues 85 & 86*

Manx, four hailed from the Manchester area and one resided in Flint.

A manuscript of 1883 survives in which appears an analysis of costs, followed by an exceedingly photogenic analysis of working expenses, dated 1885 (MS 1782c). It also mentions a Snaefell Railway as "awaiting construction", with which the company would have a junction. A formal agreement had been entered into with the Isle of Man Railway Company and accommodation was to be made available at Douglas station, whence metals were to be shared until reaching a junction at Quarter Bridge. The line seems to have targeted the coastal alignment, aiming even further south than Groudle.

The route ran through stations at Ballaquayle, Falcon Cliff, Summer Hill and Onchan (the only recognisable population centre!), then over open country via Ballameanagh, Glen Gawne (Garwick) and Laxey. The remainder to the north is not described. By the time the line reached Falcon Cliff it had, presumably, ascended some 150ft (46m) from its junction with the IMR. Of these stations, those between Douglas and Onchan were ranked as suburban (one envisages a rather sparse population of bankers and clerks as likely to patronise the 0815 to town!).

Ensuing total silence indicates a lack of response by the investing public, but the territory continued to exercise its attraction (the DL & R still had an office in Douglas in 1893-4). The tourists of the day were willing to spend eight shillings for a four-seater conveyance from Douglas to Laxey (there were also seven-seater "brakes"). In this context it should be made apparent that until Fell's Snaefell line came to be built the tourist, intent on ascending Snaefell, had to follow the River Sulby up its glen, ascending steeply at Tholt y Will and then proceed over more open ground to reach the slopes of Snaefell proper. Alternatively, he might follow the Mines Road from Laxey to the Snaefell Mine and then find his own way upwards, again over open ground, crossing the alignment of the mountain road.

Coming to the schemes of 1887-8, we encounter the Fell family and their centre-rail adhesion concept. Systems for centre-rail traction (see page 17) were not new, but in John Barraclough Fell's system — the subject of exhaustive trials both in England and in France over the period 1863-1865 — he appeared to have produced a workable technology. It was to attract the support of no less a person than Thomas Brassey (1805-1870), arguably the greatest railway contractor of the 19th century, and of equally eminent financial personalities — notably the third Duke of Sutherland. Fell attempted a final proof of his system via the construction of a 49-mile railway across the Alps barrier between France and Italy, via the Mont Cenis Pass (altitude 6,827ft (2,081m)). Constructed between 1865 and 1867, it operated, after initial problems, between 1868 and 1871. Thereupon, the whole enormous edifice was dismantled, although much of its civil engineering remains clearly visible today.

A Fell railway in Brazil, the Cantagallo (the Fell section of which opened on December 18, 1873), operated with his locomotives for its first ten years, and continued to use Fell's braking system until its closure in

1966. Here, the Fell section only extended for 7.8 miles (12.53km), a far cry from 49! A third Fell line, in New Zealand, was to be built (of three miles (4.8km) in length) and by determined efforts attained technical reliability — operating from 1878 to 1955. Fell senior meanwhile diversified into lightweight narrow gauge lines, the earliest being almost 'monorail' in their conception.

George Noble Fell (eldest son of John) had a substantial part to play in his father's enterprises, but also worked independently on railway schemes in the Isle of Man, Italy, Spain, America and England. He was a competent civil engineer and had been given quite a wide-based training. He became an

George Noble Fell, 1849-1924. (Brian Barraclough Fell)

associate member of the Institution of Civil Engineers in 1896.

Certainly, from 1887and possibly earlier, Fell junior worked extensively on these east coast Manx railways. The first — the Douglas, Laxey and Snaefell Railway — made a formal application for the Douglas-Laxey section in 1887. Its plans survive as a bound volume dated January 1888. The line followed the Peel Line of the Isle of Man Railway until a little way short of Quarter Bridge, where it climbed towards the inland part of Upper Douglas and then, heading north, crossed the upper part of Summer Hill Glen. Beyond, it passed roughly midway between the Onchan crossroads and the parish church, en route for a viaduct crossing the Groudle River, seawards of the existing road bridge. A route which paralleled the future electric tramway was then followed until the latter's alignment was joined at the present day Half Way House level crossing. Thereafter, to its Laxey terminus, the majority of the route followed was to be adopted for the electric line of 1894. The probable circumstances for this are outlined later.

In order to make compulsory land purchases the company had to secure Tynwald's sanction, and in November 1888 Fell duly appeared to this end before a special committee. The proposals were ambitious and seem to have included elements much related to his father's "railways on light viaducts" concepts. One mile of its construction (of the eight) was to be on these lines with more substantial viaducts at Groudle and Garwick, with heights of 50 and 70 feet (15.2m and 21.3m).

To reach the suggested quayside terminal at Douglas would have brought land costs to £62,000, but if parallelling the Isle of Man Railway [1] for the initial part of its course the costs reduced to £37,000. The plans were lodged in the Rolls Office on September 19, 1888 and the formal inquiry began on November 6. Fell's evidence provides an illuminating outline of his career to date, and introduced a supporting technical witness

---

[1] With which it was then to share a joint station.

A hint of the type of viaduct structure favoured by George Noble Fell can be gleaned from this example on the 3ft gauge Torrington and Marland Railway in Devonshire. (Fell family papers)

in the person of James Whitestone, who was previously an articled pupil of the Midland Railway's W H Barlow.

While governmentally approved, at this stage Fell's scheme was destined to hibernate for another three years. In the meantime the continued "developer" interest in the area produced the Douglas, Laxey and Maughold Head Marine Drive and Tramway Company Ltd, registered on September 8, 1890 with a capital of £100,000.

All seven subscribers had London addresses. Joint working with the Isle of Man Tramways Ltd (the horse-powered tramway operator) was proposed, though with no details of motive power. North of Laxey, the landscape to be traversed was one that was chiefly occupied in stock rearing, although there were periodic 'excitements' related to mining and quarrying prospects. The countryside is visually attractive but its tourist potential with a Maughold terminus seems a trifle limited!

In 1891, Fell's initial scheme of 1887-8 was revived with a new title — Manx East Coast Railways. A second book of lithographic plans survives, showing a line from Douglas to Laxey. Starting at Douglas with a station just north of the IMR locomotive shed, the line paralleled the IMR to Quarter Bridge and then followed the River Glass, crossed the road to Tromode, and climbed by sinuous reverse curves to cross the Glencrutchery stream beyond the then Douglas waterworks.

The next station was to be close to Onchan's central crossroads, after which the line descended towards Groudle, crossing the stream by a 44ft (13.9m) high bridge. A summit height of 325ft 6ins (101m) was reached just over six miles from Douglas, the route thereafter being broadly that of the electric line as built in 1893-4, but ending at the Queen's Hotel, Laxey, 150ft (46m) above datum. The total distance was eight miles seven furlongs five chains (14.4km). In this 1891 reemergence of Fell's original scheme the mention of Snaefell disappears, but the survey seems to have passed to a separate Snaefell Railway Company with an office at premises in Athol Street, still extant early in 1895.

In the "no direct connection to Snaefell" category follows Daniel Cregeen's Douglas, Laxey and (now) Dhoon Railway, whose lithographed plans exist in the Manx Museum. Although they are probably post-1890, they are the culmination of much earlier field work dating back (as earlier implied) to, at least, November 1883. From a full-scale separate terminus near the North Quay (and fronting the IMR station), it was to tunnel under the Peel Road/Athol Street junction to emerge alongside the IMR, which it then followed to Quarter Bridge. The line then turned north-east to Ballaquayle Cottage, with no gradient steeper than 1 in 50 and with bridges at all road crossings, save for a level crossing at Summer Hill Road. After a station at Onchan, close to the centre of the village, the line was to parallel the road to Laxey, crossing the Groudle River by four 80ft (29m) spans with a maximum height of 68ft (21m). Beyond here, the route followed was largely akin to that of the later electric line, but with a girder bridge to cross the main Laxey road, a viaduct of three 50ft (15m) spans across Glen Gawne (Garwick), and a summit level of 319ft (97m) which was reached after five miles five furlongs (9km). The Laxey station was, again, just seaward of the Queen's Hotel on the 150ft (46m) contour line.

The ensuing section was much more dramatic. A seven-arch viaduct 99ft (30m) high with spans of 43ft (13m) was to cross the Laxey Valley on a curve of six-and-a-half chains [1] radius — forming a virtually complete semi-circle. A mineral branch to the washing floors was to form a trailing connection just beyond the viaduct. From here, as far as the Dhoon terminus (at 442ft (140m)), the line was to climb at an almost constant 1in 31. The intended terminus, ten miles from Douglas, was actually located on the southern shoulder of Bulgham Bay where a somewhat obscure railhead development was envisaged.

Comparison of Fell's 1891 MECR survey with the alignment of Frederick Saunderson's Douglas and Laxey Electric Tramway of 1893-4 obviously suggests that much of the groundwork of the latter was taken (by agreement?) from the former. Circumstantial supporting evidence can be seen in the ensuing (early 1895) engagement by the D & LET's Alexander Bruce of George Noble Fell as surveyor for what became known as the Snaefell Mountain Tramway, and its use of Fell railway technology; albeit only for its braking provision.

---

[1] *The chain (22 yards or approximately 20 metres) is the traditional unit of measure in describing the radius of curves on railway lines.*

The Electric Tramway Company and the Provenance of the Snaefell Mountain Railway Association

By the 1890s, the essential nature of the Island's holiday industry showed change. Douglas began to acquire a succession of promenades, linked by a busy horse tramway, and places of mass entertainment (in a somewhat 'Crystal Palace' manner) which diversified the shoreline.

The economic growth of the era was vigorous and Alexander Bruce was perhaps the best example of the entrepreneurial personalities of the day. His downfall and disgrace will shortly be mentioned, but at this point the writer feels obliged to quote the late Major F C Harris who, as a small boy, had seen the impending defendants in the "Bank Trial" temporarily incarcerated in his uncle's conservatory. Major Harris was a man of exemplary candour who simply pointed out that Bruce's cardinal sin was to have been found out!

In the writer's 1993 text on the history of the Manx Electric Railway appears a relatively detailed account of the series of events which (masterminded by Bruce) brought into being the three foot gauge tramway destined, by 1894, to link the northern extremity of the Douglas promenades with the village of Laxey (1993's centenary celebrations centred on the initial trial line to Groudle Glen, opened for a short season on September 7, 1893).

This undertaking carried itself forward with visibly excellent operating results and correspondingly generous dividends. The fact that these were in part augmented by money taken from non-revenue sources was to take until the bank crash of 1900 to emerge. The dramatic events of the latter year threw the conspiratorial activities of Alexander Bruce and his business associates into sharp focus — a subject again given attention in the writer's 1993 text and (in greater depth) in Connery Chappell's *The Dumbell Affair*. Suffice to say, for the moment, that in the private grouping represented by the Snaefell Mountain Railway Association appear many of those individuals prominent in the affairs of the Douglas Laxey Coast Electric Tramway Company Ltd and its successor's manifestation as The Isle of Man Tramways and Electric Power Company Ltd.

By the end of 1894 the technology of the Douglas and Laxey line had been seen to be reliable, and the continued close association between

Bruce and its noted technician, Dr Edward Hopkinson, was a cordial one. Alexander Bruce was born at Banff, Scotland, in 1843. He served an apprenticeship with the City of Glasgow Bank and then came to a Douglas subsidiary, the Bank of Mona. When the Glasgow bank failed in 1878 he became general manager of Dumbell's Banking Company — an insular concern already secretly on the brink of insolvency. Bruce, a man of powerful character with a particularly captivating and "magic" personality all of his own, took all this in his stride. He kept Dumbells under full sail, hopefully seeing in expansion a cure for its ills, and he almost succeeded. The Snaefell scheme that we are now to describe was only one of his many endeavours. By 1892-3 he had already become Town Treasurer of Douglas and a Justice of the Peace, and he now entered into railway promotion.

Dr Edward Hopkinson was a member of an academically distinguished family who, with his brother Dr John Hopkinson (and in association with the Manchester-based engineers Mather and Platt), effectively led the UK development of electric power generation and its application to railway traction between1883 and 1896.

By the latter year the enormous growth of electric traction in the United States meant that the Hopkinson designs became virtually obsolete. Bruce, uncharacteristically, must not have been aware of the technical revolution this represented and chose to repeat 1893-4 Douglas and Laxey designs on the line he proposed to build, an "electric" manifestation of G N Fell's Snaefell railway scheme of eight (ten?) years earlier.

This said, there is also to be explained the apparent eclipse of the Douglas and Laxey Coast's civil engineer, Frederick Saunderson. In his case it appears that his absence from the scene arose simply from the fact that George Noble Fell's Snaefell Railway sat, as it were, on the shelf and "precooked"! G N Fell's willingness to have his survey exploited in this way must, in part, have been related to his continued determination to press the merits of Fell system railways. His father, now 80, had recently (January 1895) applied for yet another patent, this time for electric traction variations on the Fell railway theme.

Meanwhile, G N Fell was commissioned to survey a succession of moderate sized railway projects in various contries, most of which came to be built. However, the practice (which he shared with two successive partners) was only moderately profitable. Fell expended many hours on Fell railway schemes for Alpine routes, and for a Channel Tunnel application, none of which were to eventuate. Following his death in 1924, his son, Brian Barraclough Fell, and other family members ignited a (much regretted) bonfire of both George Noble Fell's and John Barraclough Fell's papers. It was obvious to them that the role of the Fells in railway technology had ended.

This summary of George Noble Fell artificially carries the timescale forward to 1924, but his significant connection with the Snaefell line is confined to the year 1895, other than when seeking its use for Fell locomotive trials in 1913. In returning to the early part of 1895, the Snaefell

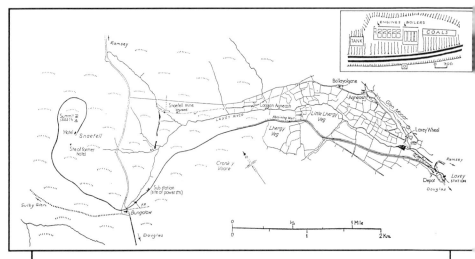

The Snaefell line with plan of the power station inset. (John C Cooke)

story can, therefore, be resumed in its mainstream context leaving the activities of G N Fell to another biographical text.

With their visitor totals and prospects completely transformed by their new electric tramway, the people of Laxey village honoured its promoters by inviting a director to open the church bazaar late in 1894. Dr Richard Farrell, a noted raconteur and IOMT & EP's most vocal propagandist, came and in his speech revealed a new ambition by declaring: "My friends, I will let you into a secret. We are going to put an electric tramway to the top of Snaefell." Bruce's new target, the Snaefell mountain (2,036ft (620m) high) stands at the heart of the mountainous northern half of the Isle of Man and is the Island's highest point. On a clear day the visitor can look out from the summit and see not only the entire Island, but also

Railway World's profile of 1896 — direct from G N Fell's survey, which is now lost. Its point of origin is the presentday car shed. (John C Cooke)

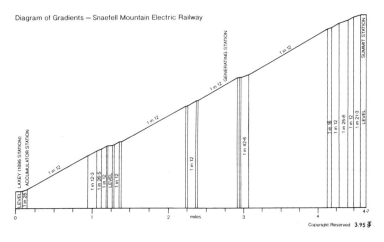

Diagram of Gradients — Snaefell Mountain Electric Railway

14

across the Irish Sea to four kingdoms; picking out the mountains of the English Lake District, the Mull of Galloway in Scotland, the hills of Anglesey and North Wales, and the Mountains of Mourne to the west, in Ireland. This was, at last, to be the location of the first mountain railway in the British Isles.

As explained in Chapter One, in 1893-4 a Snaefell Railway Company still existed, with offices at Athol Street, Douglas. Meanwhile, Fell's Douglas-Laxey survey was apparently used by Saunderson. Sections of his route appear on Saunderson's initial survey plans, of which copies were still in existence at the Manx Electric Offices in 1963-4. By 1894, Fell must have been in direct contact with Bruce, who was immediately attracted by the possibilities arising from a line up Snaefell — using the Fell system with electric propulsion. Fell's ready-made survey of 1887-8 was evidently employed, and the whole line came into being in the incredibly short time of about seven months — despite

LATER (1898) EXTENSION OF S.M.T:
COURSE OF MER. RAMSEY LINE :
EMBANKING &c (ESTIMATED FROM PHOTOGRAPHS) : 1895ᴬ 1897ᴬ
PRESENT SPOIL LIMIT (TIPPED POST 1898):
NEW TRACKS (1995) (New Workshop & Siding)

From Snaefell

Q

B

1897 EXTENSION

Road to Agneash

P R

ACCUMULATOR HOUSE 75'3" x 20' (position approximate)

former Garden

WORKSHOP (1995)

1895 CAR SHED 119' x 20'6"

NEW DEPOT (1995)

A

UP

Winch

Smithy (1995)
Amenity Block (c.1988)

Sector Plate

1895 STATION BUILDING 63'6" x 20'3"

1897 STATION BUILDING 46'6" x 17' x 8'3"

To Ramsey

Wall (1897)

Driveway

'NEW' ROAD

Vicarage Garden

Later (c1898-9) Retaining Wall

To Laxey Station

S.M.T LAXEY
SHOWING 1895 & 1897 TERMINI
(NOT TO SCALE)

Drawn by DGC 1968. Revised and inset added by JCC 1995

Copyright Reserved

TRACK LAYOUT 1995

200 metres
500 feet
100

MER.

The complex history of the Snaefell line's depot and its Laxey stations. The track A and the sector plate to the south were removed after 1896 and track B to the sector plate's site in 1897, along with track Q. The Civil Aviation Authority railcar shed is letter R, while letter P is the location of the depot's original sector plate. (D G Coakham and J C Cooke)

severe weather conditions earlier in the year.

The line avoided the usual legislative delays by being built on lands purchased or leased by voluntary agreements. There was no need for the authority of Tynwald or any other statutory power because no property had to be taken compulsorily. The land occupied by the lower end of the

15

1895 Car No 13 of the coastal tramway, taken at Groudle (A D Bailey)

line at its depot was purchased mainly by Bruce between January 26 and March 2, 1895. Higher up the mountain, the land was bought by the Snaefell Mountain Railway Association from the Trustees of the Commons. [1]

This purchase, sanctioned by Tynwald on July 9, 1895, comprised the trackbed, the site of the Summit station and hotel, the power station, Sulby pumping station and the rights of way. A 50-year lease was taken on all of the remaining land within 440 yards of the summit. The trustees were to receive one penny per passenger (minimum £260 per year) and certain levies arising from profits on the hotels.

The Snaefell Mountain Railway Association was a private grouping of Bruce and his colleagues, formed on January 4, 1895. Its named members were Bruce, J D Rogers, C B Nelson, William Todhunter, Francis Reddicliffe and J R Cowell (14 others remain anonymous).

Meanwhile, on Wednesday February 20, 1895, the first annual general meeting of the Isle of Man Tramways and Electric Power Company was held at the Strathallan Crescent offices, with Bruce presiding. Net profits were stated as £10,507 8s 10d, and the October dividend of six per cent on preferences and seven-and-a-half per cent on ordinary shares was repeated for the second half-year. Four new cars (Numbers 10-13) were on order from G F Milnes & Company for the coastal line: the electrical equipment was installed by IOMT & EP at Derby Castle. They deserve mention here as Snaefell line "look-alikes".

At this same meeting Dr Farrell, who was only allotted two minutes, nonetheless made a lengthy speech with some Manx anecdotes. His book, *Beyond the Silver Streak in Manxland — The Great Electric Railway*, was about to be published by John Heywood of Manchester and is commended as a surely unique piece of tramway promotional literature. Typically, he recited a "remarkably high encomium" (expression of praise) allegedly exchanged by two rural Manxmen boarding a Douglas

---

[1] *From 1860, the mountainous area centred on Snaefell came under control of Commissioners. The Act designated "roads" but these trackways bore little resemblance to the mountain road of today. Nevertheless, in 1895 the Highways Board required the Snaefell Association to obtain a wayleave in order to cross their road at the Bungalow.*

and Laxey car at Ballabeg one wet winter's night:

"*By gosh, Quilliam, it looks lek stepping into a fust class pub,*" said one.

"*My word,*" replied his companion, "*bud the derachthors are plucky buoys.*"

"*Garn Man; they say that every sowl on the board is from a different nation.*"

"*Lor' a massey, is that thrue?*"

"*Thrue as Gospel.*"

"*Well, that beats Owld Nick; there's not the lek of it in the unyvarse.*"

The choice of the 3'6" gauge for the Snaefell seems to have been directly influenced by Fell's early Mont Cenis experiences [1]. A double-headed bull-head brake rail was used to provide the working surfaces for a powerful calliper brake, while the flanges of horizontal guide wheels fitted below the heads of the rail. Although Snaefell relied on conventional

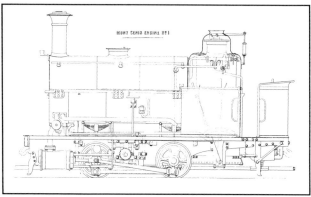

John Barraclough Fell's "Alpine" of 1863 (Canada Works, Birkenhead). This became Mont Cenis No 1. (Institution of Civil Engineers Library)

adhesion for traction, the line could have employed Fell system propulsion, as built. On the steam Fell lines, the horizontal wheels were driven by separate cylinders (or by combined motion from common cylinders) and could be forced against the rail by spring pressure to obtain adhesion far greater than would have been possible using conventional systems in which adhesion was limited by the locomotive's weight. A further refinement (post 1900), patented by engineer Hanscotte of the Fives-Lille locomotive works, was to apply pressure to the horizontal wheels using compressed air, the pressure varying with the gradient. This variant was used for the only true mountain railway built as a steam-operated Fell-type line, the Chemin de Fer du Puy de Dôme at Clermont Ferrand (1907-26).

---

[1] *He had worked there under contractor Joseph Jopling; the South American, New Zealand and Snaefell lines were all built to virtually the same gauge as the Alpine railway.*

At Snaefell, the inherent technical limitations of DC supply meant that a new generating station had to be built near the mid-point of the line to minimise the voltage drop. A stone-built power house was erected higher up the river valley on a dramatic mountainside perch, 2.8 miles from Laxey. All the equipment had to be taken out by the embryonic mountain roads (which were to be crossed on the level) before the equipment was lowered from the formation down the mountainside with the aid of ropes and tackle. The operation took 14 days, during which period a Mr Willis also erected the ten miles of single overhead line in a mere eight. Coal for the power station had to be brought up by the tramway from Laxey, and water was pumped up through a two-inch pipe from a pumping station on Sulby river, equipped with a Galloway's boiler and 4hp Tangye engine and pump.

The Snaefell power station was the most powerful generating plant yet built on the Island. The boiler room, 36ft by 43ft and 16'3" high, housed four Galloway 120lb ppsi boilers. Each was 26ft long and 6ft in diameter, with feed pumps and injectors. The 60ft iron chimney of 5ft diameter was on the other side of the line, with the flues passing beneath the track. The

boilers supplied steam to five 120hp Mather & Platt horizontal compound engines, each with a 7ft flywheel and a speed of 150 rpm; the cylinders were of 16-inch stroke, cylinder diameters being 12ins for the high-pressure one and 20ins for the low-pressure. Each engine was coupled to a 60kW Hopkinson

The impressive array of horizontal engines in Snaefell's power station. (Mather and Platt)

dynamo, the whole installation being housed in an engine room measuring 72ft by 30ft and 12' 3" high. The switchgear was mounted on a frame of polished ash.

From the power house, an underground feeder (of the type supplied by Callenders in 1894 for the coastal line) ran downhill again and supplied the overhead line at intervals of one mile. At Laxey depot, it entered a wooden battery house with 250 chloride cells and a capacity of 560 Ampère-hours; this building measured 75' 3" by 20ft and was 8' 3" high.

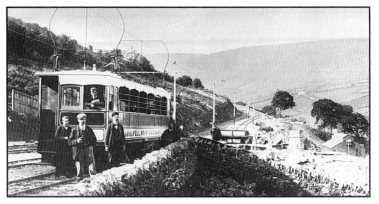

A car standing on the depot approach in August 1895, possibly pre-opening. The elaborate livery and handrail details of the Snaefell wagon are noticeable. (Manx National Heritage)

The plant was over-generous, and at a later date much of the power produced from coal, laboriously transported up 1,130ft of mountain, was returned to feed the coastal tramway through a further feeder connecting the battery house with Laxey power station.

The contractor for the Snaefell track was Mr Herd, of Douglas, and a later description of it is taken from the inspector's report. Fell and Hopkinson personally supervised their respective branches of the work. By an agreement of April 23, 1895 the Manx Northern Locomotive *Caledonia* was hired for £20 per week. It was shipped from Ramsey to Laxey in the *Porpoise* and used with the aid of a temporary third rail to reduce the gauge to the necessary 3ft. [1] MNR timber trucks No's 20 and 21 were also hired (at 3s each, per day) and the agreement specified that the engine was to be properly housed at night and that the Snaefell Association had to pay the driver 6s 6d and the fireman 4s 2d for a ten-hour day.

On Monday July 20 *Caledonia* propelled wagons carrying a party of visiting L & Y and L & NWR dignitaries up Snaefell. Concurrently, the performance of *Caledonia* seems to have been quite impressive. The Dubs works records have been found to carry an annotation of 1895 stating that the locomotive propelled a 19-ton train over a distance of four-and-a-half miles in 20 minutes. *Caledonia*'s braking system had been well designed — it only had hand brakes until the addition of a steam brake and hydraulic and mechanical Fell brakes in 1994-5. Orders had been placed for six electric passenger cars. To house these, a six-car brick shed with a curved iron roof and pits for all six cars was built at the lower terminus. This was 119ft long, 20' 6" wide and 18ft high and was to last for 99 years. This depot which, as implied, remained in use until late in 1994, was adjoined by the original and short-lived station — a 63' 6" by

---

[1] *It is possible that the line was initially laid as a single constructional line of three foot gauge (with offset centre rail) then had one rail moved out to 3' 6" gauge as* Caledonia *returned towards Laxey.*

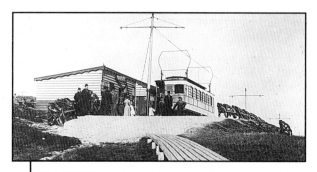

The 1895 Summit station as seen from the hotel catwalk. (Manx National Heritage)

20' 3" building approached from the public road by a long flight of steps which intending passengers had to climb. In place of normal points, the line used sector tables, that at the Laxey terminal stub being worked by a two-way winch seen in opening-day photographs. In 1897, the sector table at the summit was removed, its pit filled in, and a special type of point installed. Here a pivoted section of rail was swung across from one side to the other where the two tracks came together. The summit was provided with a wooden station building, 50ft by 13' 6", and a single-storey wooden hotel. The hotel was some 180 yards from the station building and approached by a wooden catwalk. As first photographed, in 1895, it was T-shaped in plan, but by the following year it had been doubled to become an "H", 65ft by 70ft, with a further addition to the west added by 1900.

By August 16, 1895, the work was sufficiently complete for formal inspection by Colonel J H Rich and Major P Cardew. It was not strictly a legal requirement, but the Government regarded the Snaefell line as an extension of the coastal tramway. A former Mather & Platt engineer recalled that, at 6am on the day of Major Cardew's inspection, a linesman shorted the switch panel across the already charged traction battery, converting the switchboard into a major electrical bonfire. In four hours the charred wood was cleaned off, painted with Brunswick black, and the refurbished switchgear mounted with the paint still wet; the inspector himself saying: "I haven't seen a better job!"

Colonel Rich described the line as four miles 53 chains (7.5km) in length, with a 21ft formation, of which two thirds was cut into hard ground or rock and one third built on soft material thrown out. The spacing between the tracks (as on other IOMT & EP lines) was 7ft. The "50lb" rails (actually 56lb) were fang-bolted to 9" by 4 1/2" creosoted sleepers 7ft long, and were in 24ft lengths. The Fell rail weighed 65lb per yard. The line climbed 1,820ft (555m) for 85 per cent of the distance at a gradient of 1 in 12. As shown in the profile, level stretches existed at the termini and the future Bungalow halt, and intermediately at Lhergy Veg. Most curves were of ten-chain radius but near the summit there were some of seven and five chains. J B Fell's Mont Cenis line managed 2 1/2 chains!

Apart from a desire to see more drainage, a watch kept on the formation for settlement, the provision of lamps at the stations and the fencing of "turntable" pits, Rich was satisfied. He, incidentally, explained the adoption of right-hand running as intended to keep the ascending cars on the soft part of the formation.

This only applied, of course, as far as the site of 1896's Bungalow, initially occupied by an unspecified catering structure, the "Half Way Hut". This had enjoyed a seven-day licence from an unspecified date to late summer 1895, when (on September 14) the *Peel City Guardian* reported its reduction to six days. The same paper had earlier reported the grant of a six-day licence for the Summit Hotel on August 17 (seven days had been refused). The SMRA thus planned to emulate IOMT & EP's buoyant entry to the licensed trade: this aspect of the electric railway's business survived later liquidation and continued to be significant even after nationalisation in 1956-7.

Returning to the inspection, Cardew saw the electrical equipment as basically similar to that of 1893-4 on the coastal line but, of course, the cars were higher powered. The four-motor tractive effort of 3,500lbs, set against the one-in-12 opposing forces of 2,850lbs, meant that a single motor failure would incapacitate a car. At this time, proposals for regenerative braking (in which the car motors were used as dynamos, returning current to the system) involved running downhill at 12mph (if the cars were to be unaltered electrically) and he wanted extensive proving trials before approval could be given. Cardew was alarmed at the proposed 550-Volt supply and suggested 520V as the station maximum, considering the power station to be uneconomically sited.

The voltage was evidently adjusted (probably by reducing field excitation) and the Governor gave permission for the line to open. A special car carrying "government worthies" followed on Tuesday, August 20. Opening the following day, the line carried an average of 900 passengers a day for the remainder of the season at a return fare of 2s. A Mr Carter was appointed Engineer by the parent Snaefell Association.

It is convenient here to deal with the six cars of the Snaefell line which have survived for 100 years and are still largely in their original body form. As built, the bodywork and bogies were by G F Milnes and the electrical equipment by Mather & Platt. They were to the designs of Dr Edward Hopkinson, including his third sprung adaptation of his brother's (Dr John Hopkinson) rigid bow collector (both earlier variants were used on the coastal tramway). This is perhaps the point at which to refer to the extraordinary technical survival represented by the Snaefell line's overhead suspension. That in use parallels 1893-4's on the coastal

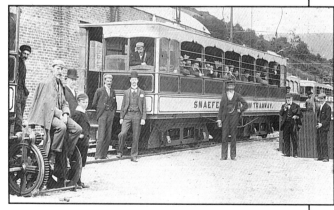

Opening day, with George Noble Fell obscuring No 1 car's identitifying digit. (Manx Electric Archives)

line. An Albert and J M Anderson (Boston) fitting was selected, with an uninsulated sleeve on the bracket arm suspending an insulated ear. The original taper steel poles had an ornamental collar and stood 110ft apart. The Hopkinson collectors, even at full reach, cannot make contact with the wire [1] where it passes through the ear. The car takes current through first one bow, then the other, with a period when both are in contact midway between poles. Ice damage on the highest sections above what is called the North Shoulder led to the early adoption of a suspension ear which is closed around the wire by mechanical means, which can correspondingly be unclamped to allow the line to be taken down, coiled and lashed to the poles. In winters when the line remained up (1954-5 when in use in connection with radio station construction and 1978-9 when left experimentally) ice accumulation took its toll. Overhead line pole renewal has been substantial over the years, and has included some of wood on the highest sections.

Returning to the cars, the form of Snaefell Nos 1-6 was basically derived from the 1894 cars on the coastal line. They were much less expensively finished, the interior being entirely of pitch pine, including the elaborately panelled bulkhead. The dimensions were: length over couplers 35' 7 1/2", height over roof 10' 4 1/2", and width overall 7' 3". The cars were ash-framed and teak-panelled, with double transverse seats for 40 and bulkhead seats for six. This was later increased to 48 by adding a single corner seat at each end. As built, they had shallow arched roofs and were glazed only in the vestibules, the six main side windows being unglazed and fitted with adjustable striped roller blinds. By April 1896 they had been fitted with sliding windows in place of the canvas blinds. In the winter of 1896-7 they gained their present roof clerestories and in 1900 they were graced with enormous advertisement boards.

Their teak and white (ivory when varnished) livery is clearly visible in the photographs. The main lettering was chocolate faced, the elaborate lining of the teak upper panel straw with a parallel fine white line. Elsewhere, fine red lines parallelled bolder chocolate ones, with graduated shading to the main letters. An unlettered garter surrounded a small fleet number on the side panel, and a brass Mather and Platt plate appeared on the sill below. End numerals matched the main title — by now *Snaefell Mountain Tramway.*

The two-motor bogies were of special long wheelbase type (6'10") to incorporate the Fell brake equipment and their two Mather and Platt 5A 25hp motors. These motors, in use until 1979, were of an archaic form with extended pole pieces and an enormous single field coil. The armatures were of the ancient series-wound type, and the techniques perfected in the early 1960s for rewinding them, using modern glass fibre insulation, were then seen as a typical revelation of Manx Electric technical skill. Regrettably, events after 1970 showed that the new method had only delayed the onset of "exponential" failures, and re-equipment took place in 1975-9.

---

[1] *This was* No 3 BWG, *with a diameter of 0.372.*

The original control system provided series-parallel working from the upper end, and series only (with five notches) from the lower end where, as most propulsion was by gravity, the simpler control was sufficient for local manoeuvres. Trials were carried out in 1895 with a car wired-up for regenerative braking, which returned up to 50 electrical horsepower to the line and saved a good deal on brake shoes. The regenerative braking suggestion was discussed in 1904 with Sir Philip Dawson, but it took another seven decades before it was adopted in the form of dynamic braking, dissipating the current generated as waste heat via resistors (rather than by adopting true regenerative braking).

The presence of a level section during an otherwise continuous descent (Lhergy Veg) made for technical complexity (passengers get the impression of an actual reverse of descent to ascent at this point).

Later engineering changes were few in number. About 1906, two stiffening channels were bolted to the lower faces of the original underframes, and the guiding wheels were relocated to a position outside the inner bogie cross-member. A rigid bogie brake screw column replaced the original type, which was flexibly jointed to a staff mounted on a platform. Almost 50 years later (about 1954) the uphill end controllers (which had become orthodox General Electric K11's early in the century) were modified to Form K12 and new GEC main switches were fitted; replacing the original Mather and Platt ones and their 0-500 ammeters. These last were superb instruments: internal inspection revealed silk-covered insulation in pristine condition.

The other three items of rolling stock comprised an unnumbered tower wagon trailer, a small unnumbered goods wagon (built in 1895 by Hurst Nelson to carry supplies for the hotel) and a coal car numbered seven and nicknamed "Maria". No 7 was a double-cab, six-ton wagon-bodied underframe of unknown date and parentage. However, its underframe carried the same rolling mill marks as those of the 1896 Douglas cable cars, and its truss rods were of standard Milnes design. This compact vehicle acquired trucks, equipment and bow collectors from a passenger car each winter (usually No 5) and took the next season's stock of coal up to the generating station. It was certainly in use in 1900, and seems most likely to be original (1895). After generation ceased at Snaefell power station in 1924 it was used only for construction work, the last occasion being some Air Ministry work at the summit in the winter of 1954-5. In 1898-9 attempts were made to secure winter mineral traffic from the Snaefell lead mine, and sections of a light railway plan by John Todd survive today, bearing the date October 5, 1899. This would have included major inclined planes. Of No 7's career, more is to follow!

Returning to 1896, the Snaefell Association proceeded to sell its line to the Isle of Man Tramways and Electric Power Company (as it had intended from the start). At the IOMT & EP Annual General Meeting on February 28, 1896, the Directors Report explained that a debenture issue was needed to finance the new Douglas cable tramway and the Snaefell line's purchase. A private meeting followed at which the Snaefell line's purchase for £72,500 was agreed. The agreement called for £32,500 in

"Maria" — drawn by John Slater, with amendments by S Broomfield and Keith Pearson.

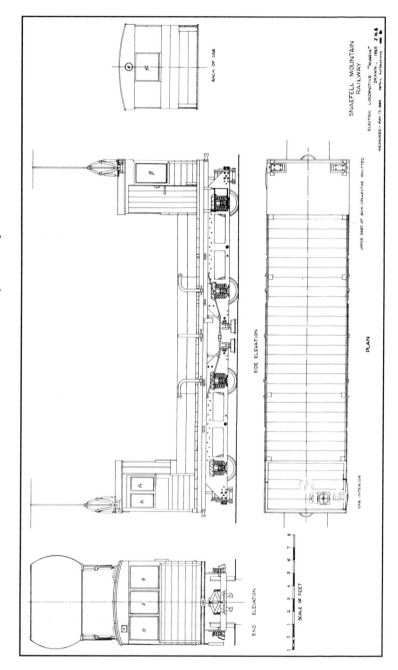

BACK OF CAB

SIDE ELEVATION

END ELEVATION

SCALE OF FEET
0 1 2 3 4 5 6 7 8

PLAN

UPPER PART OF BOW COLLECTOR OMITTED

CAB INTERIOR

SNAEFELL MOUNTAIN
RAILWAY

ELECTRIC LOCOMOTIVE "MARIA"
DRAWN — 1965
MEASURED: MAY 17, 1964
DETAIL ALTERATIONS

cash, with the remainder in equal amounts of six per cent preference and ordinary shares of the tramway company. The amount clearly included a profit to the association's members, but it later transpired that the real cost of building the line had only been about £40,000 and that the £2,000 put into the SMRA by IOMT & EP had brought a return of 100 per cent. The Snaefell Association was wound up later in 1896.

The two termini in Laxey were a good distance apart, and the long climb up to the Snaefell line's station [1] was a deterrent to visitors. In the IOMT & EP Company's Directors Report, presented on February 20, 1896, it emerged that the coast tramway had been extended in the winter of 1895-6 by a bridge across the Rencell road to a station just short of the future viaduct. This was a new single-storey building, 43' 3" by 19' 6". From here, through-passengers could walk across the road viaduct towards the Snaefell line's steps. However, by February 1897 land had been purchased alongside Dumbell's Row to bring the line to a new low-level terminus. On reaching level ground, the up and down tracks came together in a pivoted switch of the type now installed at the Summit, and a rustic station building was erected which measured 46' 6" by 17ft, replacing the larger station on the hillside. The adjoining access to the vicarage involved an enclosing ramp to the east.

The line to the depot now diverged from the downhill running line on the gradient. A special turnout of unique design was installed, with four moving sections that provided a five-stage "curve" on the turnout, complete with Fell rail. This survived until 1981, but the centre rail was not used for normal braking as the crew slackened off the rear brake when approaching the point and applied the front one immediately after passing it. These remarks apply to a descending car with its rear brake in operation in the normal manner; proceeding straight down the hill. It was obviously impossible to pass around the segmented "curve" (resulting from the diverging position) with the brake applied.

Access to the depot building was still by a sector table which survived until about 1932; Mr Lewis Gale of the MER recalled a car falling into its pit. The reason for the adoption of the sector tables and their replacing single blade switches remains totally obscure, for when later conventional point-work installations were adopted, it was self-evident that the Fell gear hung well above the heads of the running rails. Present day operating practice, with the use of the radio telephone links, presents an acute contrast with the operating rules of 1895. These were to effectively continue to be applicable until the 1980s, with an additional clause requiring a "flagman to be posted in rear" in the event of any unscheduled halt. This arose following the 1905 collision (see Page 28).

Geographically, the creation of the present joint Laxey station in 1898 arose from the coast line's Ramsey extension — opened to Ballure in 1898. The heavily engineered intermediate terminus of 1897 thus enjoyed a lifespan of but one year though its building survives — as today's Laxey

---

[1] *A 'shed' used by SMR personnel at the depot as late as 1961 was a remnant of this structure.*

The completed second Laxey terminus with its single blade switch and the highly rustic station at the right. (Manx National Heritage)

station! Elsewhere on the Snaefell line itself, operating success saw commensurate additions to the amenities as year succeeded year. The Summit Hotel was extended and in 1896 the Half Way Hut grew into a much more grandiose building — the Bungalow, a 90ft by 80ft structure of corrugated iron and timber. From here tourists were gently led to the charms of Tholt y Will and the Sulby Glen (the course of the infant Sulby river). Such was the contemporary enthusiasm for the Glens of the Island that it almost saw the construction of a Snaefell Mountain Tramway branch line to Tholt y Will, a prospect confidently referred to in company literature of 1896-7.

Dr Farrell had, by 1895-7, taken to acting as impromptu guide to those travelling up Snaefell, and at the summit would declaim:

"Here you see seven kingdoms — England, Ireland, Scotland, Wales, the Isle of Man, (the kingdom of) Man and, where is the seventh? Ah, the Kingdom of Heaven!"

As the Sulby Glen hotel is known to date from 1897 the existence of a connecting service of horse drawn brakes between the Glen and the Bungalow is self evident. Mechanised access to Tholt y Will was to achieve reality early in the new century, and Dr Farrell's role as guide was the precursor of a series of professional successors; but these matters belong to our succeeding chapter...

The Manx Electric Years

Part 1: 1902-1919

The collapse of Dumbell's Bank in February 1900 embraced the enormously over-capitalised Isle of Man Tramways and Electric Power Company. Liquidation ensued, and in a move echoing the more acute dealings of the late Alexander Bruce (who had died before the Bank Trial took place), Baron Schroeder purchased the coastal and Snaefell lines in a deal finalised on September 5, 1902. The payment received by the liquidator was £252,000. Mr Schenk, the intermediary, now promoted the Manx Electric Railway Company, which was incorporated on November 12. The new company paid "the Manchester syndicate" £370,000 for the line — a mark-up of a healthy 47 per cent.

Schenk remained involved as a Director with Messrs Kitching, Vaudrey and Greenwell. All of the latter had interests in overseas railways, and for much of its life the Manx Electric's business affairs were run from River Plate House, the London home of many South American railways. In the closing years of the company, the Greenwell family (by now with a majority interest) tolerated arrears that a more commercially-minded dynasty would have seen as ample reason for closure and liquidation. The undertaking had cost more than it was worth and the ordinary shareholders of the MER were only to be rewarded by dividends in two years of the 55 of its existence (1907 & 1913).

The new company was blessed with the services of devoted professionals who worked hard to make a going concern of their railway. In the palmy years before 1914 they repeatedly came close to succeeding.

Immediately before the record season of 1907 there had been a less rosy episode. From early in the century, the new mountain road became a road racing venue. This periodically closed the SMT road crossing to tramcars, which then ran a shuttle to and from Laxey using both tracks for

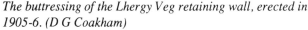

The buttressing of the Lhergy Veg retaining wall, erected in 1905-6. (D G Coakham)

27

ascent and descent (the crossover below Bungalow took until winter 1953-4 to eventuate). On September 14, 1905 a convoy of three descending cars encountered a fourth which appears to have stalled during ascent. The last of the descending trio ran into its predecessor with relatively drastic damage of the broken glass variety, resulting in the rule book change already mentioned.

Compensation payments to those injured in the accident were to

1896 Bungalow Hotel. (D G Coakham)

coincide with the extensive reinforcement of the Lhergy Veg retaining wall, but results in 1906 were still good enough to also fund new coast line vehicles, the new Summit Hotel and the purchase of the Laxey Glen gardens.

Over the years leading up to 1914, the company made strenuous efforts to technically modernise its equipment, and consequently enjoyed the benefits of AC generation and distribution.

However, on Snaefell the cars became locked in something of a time warp and their 1895 format remained substantially unaltered (they were of course only in use from Whitsun until late September).

The Snaefell line was the object of intensive promotion from 1907, largely through its involvement in "full-day tours", making extensive use of the MER's catering facilities and involving mechanised access to Tholt y Will. In July 1907 the MER brought in a motor charabanc service from the Bungalow to Tholt y Will, at the head of Sulby Glen, where it had built a large rustic tea-room. The licensing returns show two Argus vehicles up to 1913 (registrations MN 67 and MN 68), three for 1914 (the addition being a De Dion, MN 479), and two again after 1917.

The latter date seems ambiguous, as it was to be summer 1920 before two grey painted *Caledon* 27-seaters made their appearance. Possibly, these vehicles were not totally successful, as in 1926 their place was taken by a trio of smaller vehicles — blue painted Model T Fords which each seated 14. These soldiered on until 1939 when there appeared two six-year old second-hand Bedfords. The date at which the MER vehicles first ventured down to the foot of the Glen (where there was already a hotel) is uncertain. It may have been from the outset (1907) but apart from a view of one of the 1939 vehicles at the hotel all views known to the writer are at the upper entrance or at the Bungalow.

Immediately before this venture into road motors, catering arrangements at the Summit were given a major uplift by the 1906 construction of a new combined station and hotel building — a handsome castellated structure (destroyed by fire in 1982). This had a frontage of 100ft and a depth of 80ft, with a 25ft high round tower as a central feature of its facade. This was opened on August 10, having been built in a mere four

The new Summit Hotel of 1906. (FKP)

months. Once the Tholt y Will service was running, the company made extensive use of the catering facilities both at the Bungalow and the Summit to provide refreshment for the patrons of its full-day tours whose ticketing ultimately comprised a book of tear-off vouchers for each stage of the journey and for luncheon. By the 1930s No 1 Tour took passengers to Snaefell for lunch then on to Ramsey, while No 2 Tour used in-house catering at all three of the mountain locations (Tholt y Will, Bungalow and Summit).

The Tholt y Will refreshment room. (Manx Electric Archives)

The vigorous promotional activity managed to keep the obligations to MER Preference Shareholders and Debenture Holders fulfilled (which category comprised 75 per cent of the MER's stock). However, following the outbreak of war, Snaefell closed on August 9, 1914 and remained so until June 10, 1919, and coast line traffic fell acutely.

From the outset (1902), MER passenger figures for Snaefell were not separated from the entire group of lines, so that of the 700,000 carried in 1913's record breaking season one can only hazard a guess that the Snaefell line must have run to capacity (2,400 passengers) on many days.

The only major technical innovation on the Snaefell line before 1924 was the 1904 removal of one of the 1895 Mather and Platt sets and its replacement by a Kolben and Co (Prague) rotary convertor set. This operated on 330/350V (25 cycles), transformed down from the main MER AC network's 7,000V supply, having been carried up the mountain on extensions to the centre poles.

The AC provision at Snaefell placed the Mather and Platt equipment in the peak traffic only category, the staffing level being reduced to a fireman, an engine driver and an apprentice, until September 3, 1924. A second convertor of the 1903 series was then transferred from Laxey, so that the 1895 steam plant was sold as scrap. Its Galloway boilers have a surviving ghost (intended for exhibition in the summer of 1995) lately retrieved from life as a water tank at Ballacottier Farm in Middle Sheading (see page 45). The former engine room has continued in sub-station use since that date, though reduced in overall size. The boiler room is now rubble, but with a large cast iron steam pipe still in evidence. The 60ft iron chimney's base stands on the opposite side of the line, still communicating with the remnants of the flues that passed under the line at this point.

It would here be appropriate to add a note outlining how the Snaefell line became retitled as the "Snaefell Mountain Railway". A dated photograph by which the consequently revised livery (derived from the cars of the coastal line) could itself be dated remains untraced. Since the life of the original painting by Milnes was probably extended by re-varnishing, the possible persistence of the 1895 livery as late as 1914 has to be considered as an option. By c1920, the red lower panel now bore the revised title, and that above the windows became the strongly emphatic red element that is familiar today, with the waist panel still varnished and the window frames in a sympathetic grained finish. The cream painted advertising boards with their red lettering were, of course, an earlier addition.

Part 2: 1919-39

The season of 1919 had a late start, but in 1920 war-weary visitors crowded the Island and Snaefell's passenger figure totalled some 85,000. What did the passengers see? Immediately on leaving the combined Laxey station, by a single track road crossing, the car took to the right-hand track and began the curving ascent to the rear of Dumbell's Row. Next followed a fine view across the valley to the 1854 Laxey Wheel, the ridge on which stands the ancient village of Agneash, and behind them the hidden valley of the Mooar. The north-west limits of Baljean saw the car climb over a rocky spur before a brief level section and the buttressed stone embankment at Lhergy Veg.

Above here, the line traversed the unfenced land of the Commons Trustees. The view across the Laxey Valley now became increasingly impressive, and included the ruins of the Snaefell mine and then Snaefell itself, skirted by the mountain road. Most of the formation consists of a cut-and-tipped shelf, and traversing this section the car passed the mountain power station (at this date still operational).

The gradient slackened and the car left Laxey Valley to cross the mountain road, stopping at the Bungalow where the Caledons would be waiting. Here the line passed into Lezayre parish. The remaining spiral climb round Snaefell concluded what was certainly the most rewarding inland ride in the Island.

In the leaner years of the 1920s, the operating expertise of the MER management was fully exercised with arrears of debenture interest as a particular financial challenge. In 1927-28, there emerged the popular two-day Rover ticket which gave total freedom of all of the MER system but soon showed itself as over-generous. Consequently, the Snaefell facility was revised to one return journey only. On the MER as a whole, assessment of each day's traffic potential ensured that cars ran with decent loadings whatever the visitor population or the climate, and this careful management was shared by the Snaefell line.

Caring for the Snaefell fleet in the confines of the 1895 depot must have been an exacting task. Painting or varnishing were particularly challenging, and in winter 1932[1] the installation of a mixed gauge siding at Laxey made possible the transfer of complete Snaefell car bogies to Derby Castle works, using 3ft gauge bodies surviving from the 1930 depot fire at Laxey MER sheds. A detailed photographic record by the late A R Cannell survives (the last such journeys were to be in winter 1994-5). The cars were raised on traversing jacks as the mixed gauge had but three rails and a single switchblade in the easterly rail of the 3' 6" track.

A final major phase in the history of the Snaefell line's power supply

The transfer process, involving green car No 4. (A R Cannell)

began on May 1, 1935 when the island's 6,000V public supply became linked to a network of MER sub-stations with mercury arc rectification. Typically, Snaefell's sub-station now contained two 150kW Hackbridge transformer-rectifier installations, with an additional supply of 550V DC fed in at Laxey from the main MER substation. The 6,000V feed to the Snaefell station continued to use the 7,000 volt MER line of 1904. Not

---

[1] *A correction of 1930 in earlier texts.*

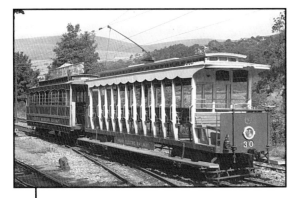

Most photographs depict Snaefell car transfers using winter saloon cars, but in 1961 this less usual combination was captured. (C L Fry)

everything had changed — the ascent of a Snaefell car continued to be accompanied by the musical note of four Mather and Platt 5As "in full cry", with the higher pitched whisper of the brush gear as a soprano accompaniment. As late as 1944-5 an archaic (1894) booster lurked in an annex at the inner end of the Snaefell car shed and saw annual service in supplying low voltage, high amperage current to dry out the motors after their long hibernation in the dank interior of the car shed.

Part 3. The Company: 1939-57

The Snaefell line closed from September 20, 1939 to June 1, 1946 and as seen by the writer in the summer of 1945 this did seem rustily self-evident. However, the war-time exploitation of the peat deposits in the area of the Bungalow by prisoner of war labour saw quite extensive use of No 5. While figures for 1946-1947 are not to hand, from 1948 Snaefell passenger figures became a matter of separate record and give a useful indication of the line's earning capability in different years. An analysis of the effects of weather on traffic simply confirm the obvious — Snaefell is essentially a fine weather ride.

The years 1945-50 were the setting for an extraordinary post-war boom era within the Island's holiday industry. Those returning to their pre-war haunts (my own parents among them) were happy to be met by an island little changed. Some military presence remained — the Royal Navy still had possession of Douglas Head until 1947, effectively sealing off the Marine Drive and its tramway. The scenes on Snaefell during 1946 when the MER recorded 1.5 million passenger journeys can only be imagined.

As part of this return to the 1939 status quo, in 1946 the MER obtained two more second-hand Bedfords, MN 8685 and MN 8686 (dated 1937). In 1949-50 the boom era drew to a close, with 1951 traffic a mere shadow of the exotic figures of 1946-7. The railway found itself faced with rising costs as its suppliers found themselves selling to a diminishing market with increasing labour costs. Road vehicle competition affected all of the MER lines, with the coach industry becoming adept at breakfast table touting. However, Snaefell traffic held up better than the circumstances might have suggested. In the figures now quoted the acute fall in

Snaefell passengers
1948-53

1948	77,000
1949	76,000
1950	60,000
1951	56,000
1952	61,000
1953	48,000

Note: The Tholt y Will service ceased after summer 1952

1953 can be seen as related to the MER overall position when an operating loss (the first since 1943) of £863 is on record.

In the mid-1950s a long established SMR institution — the flagman at the Laxey Road crossing — vanished with the death of the last incumbent, Jack Kneale. The flagman's hut position enabled a view of the hut occupied by the Despatcher and of the converging tracks where a descending car awaited its signal to proceed to Laxey station. A conventional red and green two-aspect lamp at either side of the crossing was now installed, and controlled from the Despatcher's hut until the latter was demolished in 1987 (by which time radio telephone control had been in operation for five years). The lights are now controlled from the station master's office.

The condition of the MER now reflected its increasing poverty. Track of 1893-4 on the coastal line was badly worn, with rotten sleepers hidden under a generous greensward. Cars were still well kept and the main electrical distribution system remained in good shape. Snaefell's enemy by the 1970s was corrosion. Rusting of the vertical web portion of the Snaefell rails obliged their replacement when the head had many years of wear remaining. Additionally, the Fell rail on the descending track was substantially worn.

The company was faced with spiralling debenture arrears which no foreseeable earnings could meet, especially with the inevitable trackwork reconstruction. The Island was politically still the preserve of "independents", but in Tynwald (parliament) a strong body of opinion supported the operations of the Isle of Man Railway Company (a distinctly Manx undertaking). They felt an equal instinctive coolness towards "the London company", ie the Manx Electric Railway Company.

The IMR was eagerly looking forward to a Douglas-Ramsey bus monopoly, and for a while the demise of the Manx Electric seemed imminent. However, its resident customers were vocal in their testimony of the quality of its service and its staff. At "public" level it enjoyed the support of Deemster Sir Percy Cowley, Charles Kerruish (later Sir), and an insular resident director (of pure Manx pedigree) Mr R C Drinkwater. Its joint managers of the era, J F Watson and J Rowe, were equally devoted to keeping the railway alive, and after a hectic campaign Tynwald voted for government purchase on December 12, 1956. Under climatically brilliant auspices the then Governor, Sir Ambrose Dundas Flux Dundas,

Left: Snaefell cars awaiting the morning arrivals from Douglas in 1962. (W G S Hyde)

Right: A 1955 interior. (W G S Hyde)

drove an inaugural car from Derby Castle on Saturday June 1, 1957. The political debate had perhaps been helped by an operating profit, in 1955, of £4,075.

Against this background of dwindling business and threatened closure, a modern innovation appeared on the Snaefell Mountain. The Air Ministry constructed a radio station on the Snaefell summit in the winter of 1950-51, using Snaefell cars to convey personnel and locomotive No 7 (*Maria*) in its goods haulage role (this was still in similar use in summer, 1954).

The winter 1950-51 passenger traffic on the Snaefell line meant that the detachable line on the upper section had to be left in position despite the risk of ice damage. To avoid the need for the line to be left up in subsequent years the Air Ministry, in 1951, supplied a four-wheel Wickham railcar with a Ford V8 petrol engine and a centre-rail clasp brake. This enabled the radar operator to drive to and from the Summit station.

The vehicle weighed 2.5 tons, and was fitted with Fell guide wheels in 1954-5 because of its instability in high winds. Later, in 1957, Wickham's supplied a larger four-wheel car with a 28hp Ford diesel engine; this vehicle was Fell-wheel equipped from the start and had a one ton goods portion and detachable snowplough. Both cars were kept in a separate shed at Laxey and could carry four passengers as well as a driver. Their summer operation was limited to Sunday mornings which was when the electric cars did not run. The 1951 car was to be re-engined in 1964-5. Both were in blue livery until 1966, but then became brown and yellow (for later changes see ensuing chapter).

In Government Hands 1957-95

The newly nationalised railway seemed to get off to a flying start, with a major relay of Douglas to Laxey as first priority. Board members included Mr T W Kneale, a former Indian Railways Civil Engineer, destined to be the only person who "stayed with the ship" when the first Board resigned (three years prematurely) in June 1958. An unresolved financial crisis challenged their successors (1958-62), who happily managed to achieve a more acceptable budget.

Meanwhile, the 'opposition party" in Tynwald consistantly advocated a motor road to the Summit, having recently perpetrated a civil engineering disaster (initially undetected) in their short-lived reconstruction of the Douglas Head Marine Drive. A year earlier the commodious Snaefell shelter at Laxey had been a welcome innovation.

Snaefell was given a high profile following nationalisation, and for the six years tabled below the results are self-evident:

1957	92,000
1958	68,000
1959	94,000
1960	96,000
1961	124,000
1962	111,000

The line and its equipment seemed to have an unlimited future, but the permanent way problems needed considerable remedial expenditure, which was to be secured only against considerable political opposition. John Bolton (later Sir), effectively the Island's Chancellor, constantly upheld the shining example of the recent Marine Drive conversion (this enjoyed a double-decker bus service for a short while). Mr Bolton's campaign to close both the MER and the SMR was conducted with some determination, and his ability in financial affairs was without question.

Meanwhile, a small innovation bringing substantial savings was the 1964 installation of automatic switchgear at the Snaefell sub-station, eliminating the need for continuous manning.

The first MER Board had planned a Snaefell relay commencing in 1965 and lasting for three years. By 1966 the matter was still unresolved and March 23 of that year saw a vigorous debate in Tynwald on the planned relaying, now estimated to cost £145,000. Mr Bolton again mooted his road-to-the-summit proposal, and sought to delete from the Board's 1966-7 estimates of £106,977 the first £12,500 instalment for the Snaefell task. Nonetheless, the estimates were passed, and Chairman Colebourn referred to some current successes in financial affairs, while

Dismantling Fell rail, winter 1968-9. (Manx Electric Archives)

continuing to seek to economise by closing the coastal line during the winter.

A wide-ranging debate arose from a Transport Commission report published on May 31, 1966 (which sought to close the Laxey to Ramsey section of the MER). Board matters were currently in limbo following the death of Mr T W Kneale — a new Board, now chaired by Sir Henry Sugden, took office in October 1966. In 1967 subsidence at Bulgham occupied the MER's attention, but Sir Henry had taken a Tynwald excursion up the mountain. In a subsequent vote on June 20 for essential Snaefell maintenance Sir Henry won — the writer cherishes a triumphant note from Sir Henry advising of the decision.

Work on relaying the downhill Fell rail began at the Summit in October 1968. British Steel at Workington had been persuaded to make necessary rolls and to produce successive batches of Fell rail as required. The first 100 tons were rolled during 1967 and another 100 tons came in winter 1972-3. Substantial preparations included the conversion of a Brush bogie frame (a spare from the MER) into a special rail Bender but the Fell rail bent fairly easily to the moderate curvatures required.

Fell rail chairs were made at Derby Castle with the aid of a hydraulic press, and a special measurement jig allowed correct positioning of the bolt holes in the web of the Fell rail. The later re-equipping of the cars (which introduced electric braking) has been seen by some as a reason for criticising the continued retention of the Fell rail. However, in extreme conditions Fell braking has still to be employed so that Sir Henry's "linear monument" continues to have its uses.

For the sake of completeness, the Snaefell story can be carried forward to embrace the subsequent replacement of the Snaefell line's running rails and the technical changes to the latter arising from the use of electric braking. There was first to be a period of some delay arising from the political turbulence that occupied the years between 1971 and 1974. This was when mainland consultants Transmark produced a challenging report which, again, included a close Laxey-Ramsey option (other Transmark thoughts had included a retain Snaefell only proposal). The upshot of the matter was the complete winter closure of the coastal tramway and the closure, in 1976, of the Ramsey line. When "the pudding came to be proved" in the autumn of 1976, the new House of Keys showed no hesitation in recognising that the entire Manx Electric Railway was a far more viable institution than the curtailed one whose lamentable 1976 figures were now before them.

This episode marked something of a turning point in Island attitudes towards its railways — visitors (though fewer in number) saw the Island railways as an important attraction.

The Board made a Snaefell provision of £26,000 for both 1976 and 1977, and £32,000 for each year between 1978 and 1981. The steam railway came under government ownership in 1978 and from this date an overall assessment of track priorities came to apply, with half-mile relays as a norm. Snaefell work planned for 1981-4 consequently lost out in competition for trackwork funds by the steam railway.

The elaborate Fell point at the depot vanished in 1981, with a plain track replacement and in 1982 a crossover was installed on the mountain side of the Bungalow road crossing. This arose from the rebuilding of the Summit Hotel following a fire (to be mentioned shortly) and was also accompanied by the installation of a trailing siding above the crossover, on the descending track.

When dynamic braking came to be applied to the Snaefell cars in 1977-9, rail creep was soon in evidence and anchors made from old rail were secured below the running rails and bore against the adjacent sleeper.

The second principal tale to be told in this chapter is that of the re-equipment of the Snaefell fleet. A happy side-effect of the Transmark visitation had included contact with some London Transport engineering staff, and Acton works became destined to play a major role in the programme that was executed between 1977 and 1979.

The 1970s began badly: as Snaefell car No 5 stood at the Summit on August 16, 1970, an underfloor short circuit (on the overhead side of the breakers) started a fire and rapidly reduced the vehicle to a bulkhead panel and a floor. A local joiner, H D Kinnin of Ramsey, was brought in and, in only 11 months, produced a remarkably close copy of the car in its 1895 state. It was without clerestory, but with modern windows set into its side framing. Its inaugural journey was on July 8, 1971. A change of appearance to the fleet as a whole came with the removal of the giant roof-mounted advertisement boards in winter 1970-1.

Had it not been for the onset of Snaefell motor problems it is apparent that the one-car-a-winter overhaul routine for the six-car fleet might have continued indefinitely. Until the late 1960s the Snaefell cars' running gear had resembled the machinery of a traditional ship's engine room in its spotless condition — the "newly wiped with a slightly oily rag look" was universal. Even the lubricants looked more like golden olive oil than a mere engineering product. However, this idyllic situation was to change as the decade drew to a close.

By 1973 it had become painfully obvious that a serious malaise afflicted the Snaefell fleet — according to Mr Clucas, in that year the "between rewinds" motor mileage fell to an average of 1,068. A year later the figure was down to 501, and by 1975 it had reached an abysmal 363. At about this time, the more elderly of London Transport's traction motors were managing 632,000[1]. The steps taken in the autumn of 1975 to deal with this situation have been heavily criticised by others, but the operational success of the re-equipped Snaefell cars seems to fully vindicate them (the last traditional overhaul of a Snaefell car was to be of No 4 in the winter of 1975).

MER Board Chairman John Clucas (in office 1974-6) now made a determined effort to deal with an obviously damaging situation. Utilising the London Transport (Railways) contact that was established through Transmark, the services of what became London Transport International were brought to the MER's aid (the initial consultancy was to cost £9,500).

By October 1975, after a season which had seen 55 Snaefell motor failures, the London Transport consultancy was in place and had obtained Tynwald approval for a scheme inside the £150,000 ceiling that had been imposed. By May of 1976, the consultants had found a batch of 1956-7 tramcars for sale in Aachen, Germany. There were 11 of these, but by accepting the task of removing these complete, the consultants persuaded the Germans to sell just seven. Each car had four motors of about 61 horsepower (46kW) [2] with a 24V control circuit operating electro-pneumatic contact gear. The control system was able to utilise the regenerative capacity of the compound-wound motors for service braking, dissipating the energy through rheostats. It was this capability which had most significance. Other additional braking systems included magnetic track brakes, but they were not retained. The Board Chairman and Mr Gilmore went to Aachen in June with London Transport personnel, and the deal was struck for a total of £17,500. There was a slight hitch when the car full of spares arrived in Douglas on November 12 and turned out to be empty. The material concerned was inside one of the other cars, which arrived at London Transport's Lots Road Power Station two weeks later. The intended stripping and scrapping routine was now put in hand and MER staff rescued the misdirected spares.

As the end of the 1976 season approached, there had been even more Snaefell motor failures and sometimes only one car was available for use.

---

[1] *There are some discrepancies between the SMR mileages here quoted and those in Transmark.*
[2] *The result is an increase in available power of the order of 140 per cent (240 versus 100 horse power).*

Snaefell car No 1's bogies had by now been sent to Derby Castle and were forwarded to London Transport in September. It soon emerged that the position of the new motors raised complex problems, and it would be simpler to produce replacement frames with an altered layout. Acton Works produced a pair of visually near-replicas and a later price of £58,000 was agreed for a further five sets of frames.

By early the following June, the new bogies for car No 1 were at Laxey, and the car was to be ready for trials by the 17th. At this point in time the Fell brake (still fitted as an emergency back-up) was intended to continue in partial use on the steepest sections of track, but a sixfold improvement in shoe life was confidently expected. Car No 1's body had, meanwhile, been fitted with the revised wiring and quite complex equipment of an Aachen car (including electric gongs). It made use of the original Aachen resistors which were roof-mounted above suitable shielding. The intention was to run the cars on series notches only, but in practice parallel operation has been permitted above the Bungalow — the resultant acceleration makes for an extraordinary experience when surrounded by Mr Milnes' late Victorian coachbuilding.

The wiring of No 1 provided a set of working circuit plans for the other five cars, and over the next three years these were duly dealt with. In 1979 a further £15,000 was to be spent on the provision of special high capacity roof-mounted resistances. The ex-Aachen units had a full-load duration of about ten minutes which explains the need for continued partial use of the Fell brakes. With these new units routine Fell-braking became unnecessary. Pole markings were used to indicate optimum controller settings during descent.

Car No 1's plain axle box bearings were converted to the otherwise standard roller bearing type in 1980. All the cars received larger profile wheelsets from 1988, until which time they continued to use the ex-Aachen street tramway profile, with an appreciably narrower tread.

Following the installation of the resistors, and the later stiffening work on the car bodies ending in 1987, the rehabilitation programme was effectively complete. The resulting set of six cars continues to provide a distinctive part of the Island's attractions and should offer reliable service for many years.

A regretted postscript to this account of the cars is to record the demise of the lone Hurst Nelson wagon, which collapsed "under load" in September 1981 (having lived outdoors since 1895). The re-equipment of Snaefell cars in 1977-9 saw the retention of some Milnes bogies and two makeshift wagons were now contrived from these. While 1995 has seen an even more exotic retrieval...

The other element of the Snaefell fleet, the Air Ministry (later the Civil Aviation Authority) railcars, also underwent change in 1977, with a new No 3 supplanting No 1 of 1951. Finally, railcar No 4 appeared in 1991, whereupon No 2 left the Island. This "numbering" is hypothetical but assists in interpreting the summary table overleaf.

Wickham Railcars for Snaefell

Prepared with the assistance of Wickham Rail Ltd, successors to D Wickham Ltd

	Year	Operators	Works No	Engine	Approx wt (Unladen)	Remarks
1	1951	Air Ministry	5864	Ford V8 petrol	2.5T	Given Diesel engine 1964-5, sold to MER 1977, out of use.
2	1957/8	CAA	7642	Ford 28hp diesel	2.5T	Purchased by Wickham Rail Ltd, 1991.
3	1977	CAA	10956	Perkins 4.203 litre normally aspirated diesel	3T	
4	1991	CAA	11730	Perkins 4.236 litre NA diesel	4T	Replaced 2

No's 1-3 were built by D Wickham Ltd, Ware, Herts; No 4 by Wickham Rail, Suckley, Worcester.

The new Wickham Rail Ltd railcar delivered to the CAA for use on the Snaefell line in January 1991 represented a combination of experience gained from the construction and operation of its three predecessors and the latest technology in the field. The result is a unique vehicle. Its 81 HP Perkins diesel engine drives through a hydraulic transmission (using Linde components); both axles being powered and infinitely variable speeds being obtained in both directions. The cab can accommodate a maximum of eight persons whilst a load platform at the uphill end as delivered can carry 1,500kg: it has its own crane. Particular attention had been given to sanding provision, and hydraulic braking is obtained from the transmission system. There are, in addition, hand and fail safe air brakes; the former using the Fell rail. The main dimensions are 3.886m in length, 2.35m wide and 2.58m high.

The third topic for this chapter is traffic. At different times innovations have been made, some of which have succeeded and some of which did not.

The activities of the first Board included a venture into a "new image" concept in which staff at stations appeared in a somewhat Ruritanian garb with enormously exaggerated green lapels. With this came matching trams, for the fleet began to appear (by December 1957) in a simplistic livery of green and white. Applied to the Snaefell cars, the effect was particularly "garden shed", and only No's 2 and 4 of the mountain line came to be so treated. The practice had ceased by 1959 and when No 4 went down from Laxey to reassume its normal paint style, in September of 1963, this bizarre episode became history.

A more acceptable "brave try" was the purchase of two Leyland Cubs which were formerly owned by Douglas Corporation (CMN 709 and DMN 585, dated 1938 and 1939) and were placed in service on the Bungalow-Tholt y Will run in 1957. In 1958 they became involved in an even more ambitious IMR/MER combined tour, but this did not achieve any great success. The following year they remained idle until they made a final appearance running a shuttle service from Ramsey MER station to an agricultural show at Lezayre on August 7, 1959.

The Board had elected to demolish the Bungalow (this took place in 1958) but significantly refurbished the Summit Hotel in the same year. The Bungalow site became occupied by a diminutive public shelter and conveniences, while the station-master continued to occupy the small booking office of 1895. This was demolished in 1984 and in the following year a former Isolation Hospital building (previously in use at Laxey) appeared in which the Traffic Department established an outpost. Except on race days, the railway now use the TT Marshal's office for booking purposes — car-borne tourists now ride from Bungalow in significant numbers.

In 1958, the hotel's souvenir shop was also re-vamped, and for a number of years returned good profits. When the TT grandstand at Bungalow was erected (1963) the provision of a footbridge allowed cars to run a shuttle to and from the Summit so that the railway operation was no longer curtailed by the races. This structure has been damaged by road vehicles on several occasions, and a scheme for traffic lights continues unrealised.

In 1962-3 a taped commentary was provided in the ascending cars and had moderate success, but if the car suffered delay it became conspicuously out-of-step with the scenery. A more practical step came with the fitting of headlights on the roofs of cars Nos. 2 and 3 in 1978. This

Green Car No 2 at the Bungalow in 1961. (J H Price)

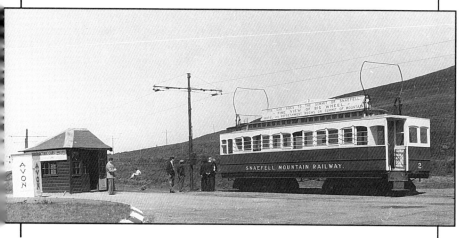

meant that "specials" might be run in the evening. A Snaefell summit sunset can be a memorable experience.

The adoption of radio telephone control has much simplified operations, but its 1982 inauguration was followed by its elimination for two complete days when, on the night of August 5, the Snaefell Hotel was destroyed by fire. The Snaefell line closed until August 9 and (in contrast to 1905) rebuilding work took until May of 1984.

Following the installation of radio control, a traffic notice imposed new operating rules pending the 1980s revision of the 1926 rule book (second edition 1989). The Snaefell line section includes specific controller positions to be adopted at different points so that both ascent and descent (using electric braking) are closely controlled.

A topic not dealt with up to this point is the service pattern on the Snaefell line. For many years the departure of a staff car from Laxey at around 8.45am allowed the mountain sub-station to be switched on and gave the hotel staff a decent interval in which to prepare for the day's arrivals. Today, the Laxey originating staff journey reaches Bungalow rather earlier, where the majority of the hotel staff have gathered (using their own transport) and where fresh provisions like bread are awaiting upwards transport. The first service car is at around 10.30am. At the other end of the day, when the line is busy, the last descending passenger car is passed by a staff car sent up to allow their return after the extra time has allowed them to clear up after the day's operations. On quieter days the last car down waits until it is apparent all visitors have been gathered and the staff join them on the descending journey.

As there has sometimes been doubt about the need for the cars to operate after mid-afternoon (on a quiet or inclement day), the decision has been made to specify the 3.30pm departure from Laxey as the latest guaranteed run of the day. Summit descent times can extend to as late as 6pm.

To complete our tale, there follow some passsenger statistics extending the record into the 1980s and the early 1990s. Between the last quoted figure (1973's 61,000) and the 1978 re-commencement which follows, the difficult years attending the Snaefell re-equipment task must have at times lowered performance (when the cars available for service could not match demand) but the figures now to be quoted are free of any external influences as good vehicle availability applied throughout. The real determining factors are of course the visitor arrivals and the weather.

The favourable results of the celebrations of the Centenary of electric railway operations in 1993 are self-evident. Present efforts by Isle of Man Railways to give due recognition to the 1995 occasion are the subject of a postscript.

Passenger Figures
1978 - 1993

Year	Island Arrivals May-Sept (1000s)	Snaefell Passengers (1000s)	Passengers/ Arrivals (Percentage)
1978	531	96	18
1979	635	145	22
1980	569	114	20
1981	457	100	22
1982	414	86	21
1983	413	100	24
1984	378	102	27
1985	351	93	26
1986	339	82	24
1987	334	86	26
1988	328	91	28
1989	323	86	27
1990	326	76	23
1991	299	69	23
1993	293	93	32

Milnes' 1895 enamel builder's plate, (3.75ins overall). (J C Cooke)

Postscript

Spring 1995

The experience of enhanced business generated by the 1993 centenary celebrations of the *Manx Electric* obviously pointed to the possibilities inherent in the succeeding 1995 Snaefell centenary. Looking back to 1993, Robert Smith and his team produced some quite remarkable attractions, including some wonderfully nostalgic moments listening to the curious murmurings of the 1898 Electric Construction Company cars. One element of the 1995 events is even more "Jurassic Park" in its

The new Snaefell Mountain Railway depot at Laxey, March 1995. (P H Abell)

impact, for from the hidden recesses of the Derby Castle have been resurrected four Mather and Platt 1895 motors, some ancient control gear and from Laxey a pair of Milnes bogies.

By way of superstructure, the long-asleep carcase of *Maria* has been rescued and substantially rebuilt, allowing us to savour the sound of a quartet of Mather and Platt No 5A's once more. *Maria* will also receive mountings capable of connection to three foot gauge bogies so that it will have a future role as a much-needed works car. The Manchester Museum of Science and Technology has kindly loaned a fifth motor — just in case.

Equally exciting, and again extending a process initiated in 1993 (when IMR No 4 hauled electric railway trailers to the Dhoon Quarry sidings from a special siding just north of Laxey station) is the rehabilitation of the 1885 Manx Northern 0-6-0 *Caledonia*, which is to return to the Snaefell line and will operate above the Bungalow road crossing. A siding to accommodate *Caledonia* and its carriage has been added to the ascending track opposite the existing downhill works siding. Subject to special braking trials now in progress it will propel passenger stock — obviously a fourth rail has been laid to permit this operation. Truly a centenary to remember.

The structural preparations have included the demolition of the 1895 depot and the erection of a wider replacement, flanked by a workshop road which will eliminate the excursions by Snaefell stock to Derby Castle. Two Snaefell Cars (Nos. 1 and 4) have spent the1994-5 winter at Derby

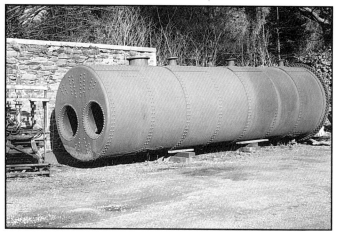

*A Snaefell boiler rescued from the farm at Ballacottier —
now at Douglas Railway Station. View is from the flues end,
at the firing end the grates remain in position but the
furnace doors are missing. (David Lloyd-Jones)*

Castle, while the other four (including the bogies of No's 1 and 4) temporarily resided under a plastic tent erected in Laxey station. Nos. 2, 5 and 6 first of all inaugurated the 1995 International Railway Festival, by conveying some 210 passengers up to the Bungalow on January 2. A special postage stamp was issued on February 8, 1995, and a centenary brochure has been published.

The author hopes this account of the Snaefell line will (in its own way) add to the appreciation of what is a most uniquely Manx institution. Being a Mancunian by birth, it is especially pleasing to look forward to seeing Mancunian technology of yesteryear once more still "alive".

*Car No 2 at Bungalow unloading for the New
Year climb — January 2, 1995. (P H Abell)*

A Ride Up Snaefell

This description of the tramway route should be read in conjunction with the scenic highlights described in the following walks.

Trams leave Laxey station from a separate line to the Coast Tramway. The gauge is different, but you will notice a linking siding and a short section of dual gauge track. This is where Snaefell cars were fitted with temporary bogies for transport to Douglas for major maintenance, up until 1995.

The track is single line leaving the station and gently climbs to cross the main Laxey Ramsey road parallel to the Manx Electric Railway. Once across the road the track is level for a short while as it passes the site of the 1897 terminus. It diverges into double track and the climb proper begins. Ascending cars unusually take the right hand track. The original Fell line starts here, although it is now used only for emergency braking and guiding the horizontal Fell rail wheels of the bogies.

The first section of the climb is at a gradient of 1 in 25 as far as the turnout. This gives access to the present depot and the site of the original station of 1895. The track immediately steepens to the overall ruling gradient of 1 in 12, maintained for almost quarter of a mile. It was considered to be the steepest practical for the tramway and remains to this day close to the limits of adhesion for normal traction.

It is not too difficult to imagine what the original contractors were faced with when building the line because little has changed. As the line left Laxey, Dumbells Terrace was there below it, the Great Wheel was there, but there would have been leadmining activity.

Laxey was a boom town and although just starting to experience a downturn in its fortunes it was still by far the most prosperous producer of silver and zinc blende in the British Isles. One feature that they would have noticed would have been the waste material from the mines, which provided a man-made mountain of waste in the upper part of the washing floors opposite the houses in Dumbells Terrace.

The line thereafter passed through agricultural land, which until recent times had been largely intack (that is land taken in from the commons and fenced). Traces of this can still be seen at Lhergy Veg, where the line eases its gradient slightly as it swings to the left and perches on a ledge above the Laxey valley a little over a mile and a half from Laxey.

Here the line is constructed on the cut and fill principle and after a short distance at 1 in 20 the line runs level — although giving the appearance of going downhill. It is accentuated by the following resumption of climbing first at 1 in 20 and then at the maximum gradient as it leaves Lhergy Veg. The line entered onto common land and the original promoters of the line were able to acquire the whole of it for the track all the way to the summit, with one small exception, from the Common Lands Board.

Prior to the 1860 Disaforresting Act many portions of the mountain land had been enclosed under licences issued by the Lords of the Island, such as the intack referred to earlier. After 1860 the control of the mountain land was vested in Commissioners and without that event it would have almost been impossible for the tramway to have been built. If such a venture was promoted now, I doubt whether it would be built. Fortunately it was a case of the promoters being respected men and being in the right place at the right time. Once on common land, construction was able to proceed at a rapid pace without the need for fencing the line and it remains unfenced where it passes over common land.

The line is built at Lhergy Veg on the steepest slopes of Cronk y Vaare, and to achieve any sort of ledge the line had to be cut into the side of the hill. It is here that the greatest engineering work was undertaken. Because of the steepness of the slope, the low side of the track had to be supported on a masonry wall. This is the area where the slip occurred in 1905 and the original wall had to be supported by a considerable number of buttresses built over a two-year period.

Leaving Lhergy Veg the line climbs at the maximum gradient and into easier going. At two and a half miles the line swings further left and approaches the site of the midway power station quarter of a mile from the Bungalow halt.

The gradient of the line eases to 1 in 25 as it approaches the Bungalow and crosses the Snaefell Mountain Road on the level. This was the only parcel of land that the tramway could not purchase on Snaefell and they had to negotiate a wayleave to cross the road from the Highway Board.

The Bungalow halt is almost three miles from Laxey and is at an altitude of 1,350ft. Here the line is on the saddle between Mullagh Ouyr and Snaefell and has just crossed from the parish of Lonan into the parish of Lezayre.

The line is now ascending Snaefell, starting from the Bungalow at a relatively easy gradient for the first hundred yards but it is quickly back to 1 in 12. The line is almost heading west at the Bungalow but soon swings northwest and then northeast, passing through another minor rock cutting as it follows the north shoulder of the mountain.

This is the most exposed section of the line and the overhead is removed in the winter to avoid the risk of damage from winds — often in excess of one hundred miles an hour. The line continues round the shoulder to end up heading south west with the spiral almost complete.

With the Summit Hotel in sight the gradient eases to level and the fell rail stops. At the end of the line the two tracks join again to allow the trams to change tracks for the descent with the unusual, if not now unique, single blade point still in use after one hundred years.

The line has climbed to a height of 1,986ft just 50ft short of the summit in four and a quarter miles.

Walks Exploring the Snaefell Railway

The following four walks are all designed to give anyone of average walking ability a different view of the Snaefell Mountain Railway and, at the same time, whet their appetite for perhaps some more adventurous exploration of the Isle of Man.

Good substantial boots are essential because of the nature of the ground over which the walks pass.

All of the walks assume a start at Laxey Electric Railway Station and use either the Manx Electric Railway or the Snaefell Mountain Railway in the itinerary and contrive to finish back at Laxey Station.

To get the best from these walks it is recommended that they be done on good clear days.

Note: The sketch maps which accompany the walks in this book are intended for a guide only. The publishers strongly recommend that walkers also carry the OS *Landranger*, sheet 95. Better still is the 1:25,000 scale Public Rights of Way and Leisure map, published by the Isle of Man Government.

The view of Laxey Wheel from the tram as it leaves Laxey. (Stan Basnett)

1. Bungalow to Laxey

3 1/2 miles
2 hours

A ride on the Snaefell Mountain Railway, taking in views of the whole Island, and a sneak into the past on the way back down.

We start the first of the four walks associated with the Snaefell Mountain Railway by taking the tram from Laxey station to the Bungalow halt.

If you haven't already travelled on the Snaefell line then there is a treat in store. Be sure to sit on the right hand side of the tram because this is where the best views are as far as the Bungalow halt, which is the only intermediate stop on the line. Between the Bungalow and the summit the panoramic views around the Island are on the other side as the line winds its way around the Mountain.

For our trip we are going to travel up the south western side of the Laxey valley, which is a classic glacial valley with its wide, flat bottom and steep, rounded sides. Our walk takes us back to Laxey down the opposite side of the valley.

View down Laxey overlooking the double-walled magazine near Snaefell Mine. (Stan Basnett)

The tram leaves the station and crosses the main Douglas to Ramsey road alongside the double track of the Manx Electric Railway. Once on the reservation, the Snaefell track splits to a double track and unusually the ascending cars travel on the right hand track.

The roofs of the houses in Dumbells Terrace fall away below us as we start the climb, passing the car shed and the site of the original station on our left.

Now look to the right as The Great Laxey Wheel comes into view. We shall see it again as we walk back to Laxey, but if you have a camera be ready because this is the classic view of the wheel with the arches carrying the pump rods into Glen Mooar behind the wheel. This is the glen where the ore was first found and which led to the development of the mines in the area that produced copper, zinc blende, lead and silver in vast quantities.

The climb continues through the fields of North Baldrine farm for a little over half a mile before swinging left to open up the true splendour of the Laxey Valley. The line is now perched on a ledge on the side of Cronk y Vaare and surprisingly runs level for a short distance to the Lhergy. It clings to the side of the mountain supported by a retaining wall built in 1895. The massive stone buttresses were added in 1906.

As the line passes Lhergy Veg the climb is soon resumed, and we shall see the extent of this civil engineering work to good effect when we are on the other side of the valley. Just below us, on the opposite side of the valley, is the road down which we shall be walking past the ruined farm of the Laggan Agneash.

The tram next passes the site of the original power house for the Snaefell Railway. A little further and we cross the Snaefell mountain road to arrive at the Bungalow, where we shall get off the tram and start our walk.

Cross the road, taking care with the traffic which tends to speed on this stretch. Go through the opening in the mountain fence, where the tram crosses the road, being careful to avoid any trams. Just walk a few steps down the left hand side, crossing the cattle grid on the tram track, and go onto the mountain land. Back track on the mountain side of the fence to the corner fence post and cross the short boggy area to start the walk.

There is no track to follow but with care we should not find it too difficult. We head off on a bearing of 80° which is heading for the saddle between Clagh Ouyr and Slieau Lhean on the skyline ahead of us. This will take us downhill alongside and to the left of a deep gully which forms one of the tributaries of the Laxey River. On our right, across the gully, is the line of the tramway and the site of the power station. Be careful as we draw alongside the power station site as we have to pass between one of the numerous boggy areas and the edge of the gully.

Now we are on the open hillside and moving away from the deep gully. As more of the valley below us comes into view, we aim for the clump of trees that just start to emerge and our heading comes round to nearer 70°. The small plantation is on the hillside above the head of the main shaft serving the Snaefell Mine and it is there that we are going, avoiding the boggy places on route.

Gradually the surface remains of the mine come into view. Can you just see the top of the chimney at the mine? If you can then line that up with the next to last overhead electricity supply pole coming up the valley and carry on until you come to a stream in another deep gully.

This stream starts on the side of Snaefell and is a further tributary of the Laxey River. You can be sure it is the right one if you look up the mountain because you should see the retaining wall holding up the mountain road at the Graham Memorial.

Just below us, and across the gully, are a number of ponds retained by an earth and stone structure. These collected and stored water for a wheel at the mine which was almost as large as Laxey Wheel but, alas, was dismantled when the mine closed.

We shall walk along the top of this wall to the mine area. To get to it we must follow the right hand side of the gully downhill until we are below the retaining structure. You can see it quite plainly as quite a substantial stone buttress. At this point the stream is quite narrow and there is an easy crossing on an exposed rock. There are other ways to cross which look tempting but I can assure you that you will get into difficulties if you try them!

Scramble up onto the top of the structure and you will find it wide and easy to walk on with just one or two places to clamber between the ponds. They are all overgrown now and present a fatal·trap to the unwary sheep that stray into them. If you look behind, you will see various leats running round the contours to collect water for these storage ponds and you can also see how they collected water running down the surface of the mountain.

Walk

1

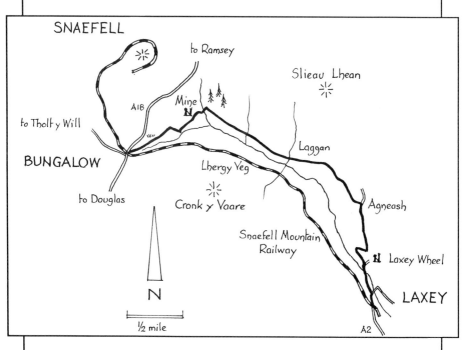

As you get closer to the chimney, which we have had in our sights all the way, you will come to yet another gully. There is now only one pond left between us and the mines chimney and just across the gully, partially hidden in the bracken, is the double-walled magazine where the explosives for the mine were kept. Don't cross this gully. Instead walk down the right hand side of it on the turf a short distance to a track which skirts the

Walk
1

top of the spoil heap. Turn left and follow it round to the road by the large house that used to be the mine captain's residence.

The workings we pass are a mixture of the masonry from some of the original buildings and brickwork from a venture in the 1950s to reclaim minerals from the waste. Behind the steel doors are the flotation tanks used in this business. Don't walk on the material behind them – it is not safe.

The original mine was started in 1856 following the discovery of the lode in the stream bed. The mine had one main shaft which reached a depth of 171 fathoms (1,026ft) with eleven levels. The mine working extended almost three quarters of a mile underground.

To give you some idea of the scope of these workings, the northerly extent of the mine reached a point 540 fathoms (3,240ft) from the shaft. On plan, and taking account of the heading of the workings, this would place it on the side of Snaefell near the Black Hut on the Mountain Road where there is a dyke like depression, but some 1,280ft below the surface. The shaft, like all in this area, was inclined and not vertical making operation of the mine difficult for winding gear and the only practical access was by ladder. The mine, although reasonably productive, was closed by 1908.

In May 1897 there was an accident at the mine in which 20 men lost their lives. A candle had been left burning at the end of the previous week's shift and it had set fire to some timbers in the 130 fathom (780ft) level. With little or no air over the weekend to support combustion the timbers had smouldered filling the workings with poisonous gasses, mainly carbon monoxide, and the miners had literally climbed down into this and were overcome before word reached the surface.

It is difficult to understand the conditions under which these men worked, not only the privation but consider the location. Imagine walking from Laxey or further in pouring rain and a gale of wind to climb down into a dark underground tunnel to do a days work, with only the light of several candles which you had to provide for yourself!

Enough, let us turn our back on that and head off towards Agneash and Laxey down the stoney road which we saw from the tram.

The tram track can be clearly seen on the right hand side of the valley perched on its ledge. Slieau Lhean is above us on the left and Laxey River with almost all its tributaries united is in the floor of the valley below us.

Eventually we come to the ruined remains of the farm buildings of Laggan Agneash — a bleak place to farm. Look up at the tram track and you can now clearly see just how massive the retaining wall is at Lhergy Veg.

As we cross what appears to be a bridge look up to the left at the beautiful waterfall at Laggan Agneash, which literally means the hollow of Agneash. It is water which came down here and the other tributaries in 1930 that caused such mayhem in the lower part of Laxey and almost crippled the Manx Electric Railway.

A short climb brings us to the farm at Ballayolgane and into the village of Agneash. Follow the road downhill on the south side of Glen Mooar. It is in this glen that the lucrative lode was found that spawned the Great Laxey Mines.

Walk

1

Although second to Foxdale as a producer of lead ore, the output of zinc blende from the Laxey mine was greater than any other mine in the British Isles. Indeed some years it was greater than all the other mines combined. The most lucrative years occurred from 1868 and reached a peak in 1875 with production of zinc blende reaching 11,753 tons and lead 2,400 tons, with silver production at 107,420 ounces. All this 20 years before the Snaefell railway was built! The decline in production started from 1892 onwards until the closure of the mine in 1929.

You can see some of the mine buildings as we continue down the road to the village. Can you see the ruined building on the hillside opposite? That is the remains of Dumbells Machine House which served Dumbells shaft, the deepest of the five main shafts, the bottom level being 1,610ft below sea level.

Soon the Lady Isabella (Laxey Wheel) comes into view as the road twists its way downhill. You can also see a large ruined building on the other side of the valley. It housed a beam engine which provided pumping and winding facilities for both Welch and Engine shafts. The tramway on the opposite side of the valley is now much lower and closer to us. The Agneash Road joins Mines Road just below the wheel and now if you look left you can really appreciate its size. Remember it was completed in 1854 without the aid of tower cranes or any of the modern aids we take for granted.

Turn right and continue into the village. As we cross the stone bridge by the engineering works we pass the entrance to the Laxey Wheel and the Mines Experience. I have deliberately avoided too much explanation of the mines because I would recommend that you go and see for yourself and marvel at the labours of those men. There are good paths around the most interesting areas together with descriptions of each building and their function.

The tram station is down the road another quarter of a mile and we walk past the former miners' cottages in Dumbells Terrace. The Snaefell tramway runs behind the houses on the final part of its descent into Laxey.

The finish of our walk is in the Mine Captain's House, now the Mines Tavern at Laxey station, whilst we wait for our tram. As well as taking well earned refreshment, you should look at some of the amazing photographs taken inside the mine by the Manx Mines Research Group which are displayed on the walls.

2. Snaefell and Beinn y Phott

3 1/2 miles
2 1/2 hours

Ideal for walking off refreshments taken at the Summit Hotel. Needs fine weather to fully appreciate the views.

We are going to take the Snaefell Mountain Railway all the way to the summit before starting the walk. Don't think that because we are starting at the top that it will all be downhill, that would be too easy! The walk will finish at the Bungalow and we shall return to Laxey by tram.

This time pick a seat on the left hand side of the tram and once we pass the Bungalow Halt the views will all be on your side.

Leaving the Bungalow we are on the mountain and opposite is the bulk of Beinn y Phott (1,791ft) — yes, we are going to the top of it! I told you it wasn't all downhill.

As the tram swings round the mountain, views open up over the western hills with Sartfell, Slieau Freoghane and Slieau Dhoo forming the backdrop to the Sulby Reservoir, which was completed in 1983 to serve the increasing demand for water for the whole Island.

We are getting higher now and our view north is dominated by Slieau Managh and to its left Mount Karran. The view of the northern plain opens up even more before we swing round and the tram quickens as the gradient eases. The scene now is of the North Barrule Ridge with North

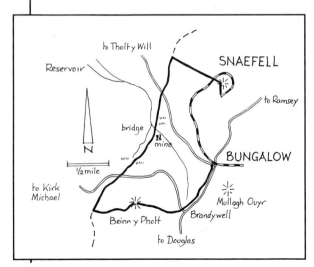

Barrule, the Island's second highest mountain (1,854ft), and its pointed summit clear in the background and the ridge to Clagh Ouyr in the foreground. This is the route of our fourth walk and to my mind the best on the Island.

Our final view as we approach the summit is almost due east down the Laxey Valley, which was the subject of our first walk. Now you can see its classic glacial form.

Let's take some refreshment at the Summit Hotel before starting off on our walk and don't forget to look at the most unusual pointwork controlling the single station siding.

If we are lucky, today may be one of the days that the steam locomotive *Caledonia* is operating on the section between the Bungalow and the Summit and we should be in the best place to see it.

Well off we go. First up the concrete path to the Trig point, which is off the path leading to one of the communication masts that dominate the summit and are so essential to modern life. We are going to head off on a bearing of 310°, aiming to the right of Slieau Dhoo and, if you can see it, the Crown Gate on the Druidale Road. We will be able to adjust the direction we want to take as soon as we start to descend and the Sulby Reservoir becomes visible below us. Be careful, the first bit of our descent is a bit steep and stoney — watch where you put your feet.

The assumption is that it's a fine clear day and, in truth, this walk is not worth doing if it isn't reasonably clear. By the way, did you notice the handrail by the path leading from the hotel to the CAA radio mast? Well, it wasn't put there for us. It is essential for the engineers who have to service the equipment all year, often in winds approaching 100 mph.

We very soon come to the tramway which we have to cross. If you have your camera this is a good place to wait and photograph the next tram in a good location — the stunning background scenery puts the tram in its proper setting as a Mountain Railway. Do you see the extra rail on the inside track which has been laid for the steam train and the centenary celebrations? If you weren't already aware, the gauge of the Snaefell Railway is 3' 6" whereas the electric and steam railways have a gauge of 3'.

Cross the track and continue down the open mountainside until we join the Millennium Way (one of the Island's long distance footpaths). We join it at the corner of the stone wall and earth dyke that forms part of the Cleigh yn Arragh — an extensive ancient earthwork.

Now is the time to adjust our direction if we have wandered off course. It is a fairly obvious landmark and when we get to the corner we shall follow it to the left until it joins the Tholt y Will Road. As we walk along the top of the earthwork there ahead of us is Beinn y Phott.

Recent forestry work has obliterated the footpath near the road and it is not possible to follow the distinctive Millennium Way markers. In fact, when you get to end of the wall cross the river and make the best way you can to join the new forest track by the side of the Bailey bridge. Alternatively skirt the top of the bank by the track and join it by the second gate. The easiest option then is to follow the track to the Tholt y Will road.

We cross the road and continue to follow the waymarkers down the mountain, aiming for the circular spoil heap on the other side of the valley. You don't have to go through the bog — the path skirts the edge of it. Once you reach the end of the bog strike downhill to the fence which can be easily crossed by a stepping stile.

*View over Colden and Carraghyn from the top of Beinn y
Phott. (Stan Basnett)*

The path is clearly defined now to an arched stone bridge which was
built and used by miners, who opened up a trial in the valley seeking a
continuation of the Laxey lode. Although a shaft was sunk, it was unpro-
ductive and the mine was closed in 1867.

As we cross the river over the bridge you can clearly see the visible
remains of the mine up the valley. If you look back the way we have come
you might just be able to see the stone wall of a sheepfold which was to
our left as we came down the hillside.

Now we start the serious uphill bit, walking up the left hand side of the
gully which we could see on the way down. You can avoid the bog that con-
fronts you and follow the path round the edge of it to the top of the bank.

The gully has a name on some of the older maps that crops up many
times on gorges or gullies like this. It is called Glion ny Maarliagh (glen of
the robbers). This stream is fed from the huge peat bog on the slopes of
Beinn y Phott. In earlier times it was one of the main sources of fuel for the
residents of Douglas. A study of the roads serving these ancient turbaries
is a fascination in itself.

We climb up the left hand side of the gully skirting the edge of it all the
way up and following the waymarkers which, although sparse, give the
best route to follow. Pause and take a look back towards Snaefell and
across the valley, looking at the route we have just taken.

Now you can see the sheepfold that I referred to at the bottom of the
valley. It is almost certainly the largest structure of its kind and is clearly
very old. It appears on the survey of the Island carried out circa 1865.

Carry on uphill and you can see that we are on the northern slopes of
Beinn y Phott. You might also be able to just make out the present day
peat digging which is permitted under licence. We have to cross a side
gully of Glion ny Maarliagh and if you look carefully you might make out
the next waymarker.

Yes, we do have to go through the bog this time — there really is no alternative. Take care and try to follow the track worn by others. You should pick up the waymarkers and follow them up to the Brandywell Road. If not then look for the signpost on the skyline and aim for that. With a bit of luck we should pick up the line of the old turbary road which curls round to the Brandywell Road.

Now we are on part of what was originally the "via regia", the oldest chronicled road in the Island. The track is quite easy to follow between its earth hedges. It flattens out after a while and skirts left as it crosses the saddle between Beinn y Phott and Carraghyn before starting to descend.

Be careful here because you will have noticed that Beinn y Phott is now well to our left and we have to reach the top of it. Don't worry, we are looking for the easy way up. A stone surfaced track joins the one we are on and we shall follow that to the left for about 60 metres looking for a very rough, poorly defined track, leaving to the left by a Forestry sign prohibiting vehicles from using it.

You will soon become used to following these old tracks and despite this one at first appearing to lead you away from the summit it curves back and is very easy to follow, with only the last few metres providing any challenge. You want to try finding it in the Manx Mountain Marathon at Easter time with visibility down to ten metres and a sprinkling of late snow on the ground!

Now we have reached the top of the Island's fourth highest hill and the view of Snaefell is worth the effort. You can see the tram track climbing from the Bungalow quite clearly. The Mountain Road can be seen climbing from the Bungalow to Brandywell which is the highest part on the TT Course. Follow it round and you will see it almost as far as the corner known as the 33rd Milestone. Beyond in the distance is Douglas and on a clear day you will be able to see as far as Langness. There is also a good view back the way we came over Carraghyn, Colden, Slieau Ruy and Greeba.

The track down to Brandywell Corner is fairly easy to follow and you more or less aim for the yellow walls of the cattle grid near the TT shelter at the junction of the Brandywell Road and the Mountain Road. If it should be misty a bearing of 105° should get you down to the cattle grid and the road.

Once at the road we only have to walk the half mile to the Bungalow and our tram back to Laxey. Instead of walking on the Mountain Road it is much quieter to walk on the mountain itself. Go through the gate behind the shelter, making sure you shut it behind you, and follow the roadside fence all the way to the Bungalow. You will find a kissing gate at the other end which gives you easy access onto the Tholt y Will road.

The tram stop is just across the road.

3. Slieau Ouyr and Slieau Lhean

4 1/2 miles
3 1/2 hours

A walk with plenty of bogs and streams, ending at the Motor Cycle Museum, which tells the story of the Island's famous TT races.

For this walk we shall take the tram to Glen Mona. If you are not sure where it is ask the conductor and he will make sure you get off at the right place.

There is a track opposite the stop which leads uphill to the main road and the Glen Mona Hotel. Cross the road and you will find the track we want to take just to the right of the hotel. Follow it uphill and go through the gate across the track. The track is no longer surfaced and becomes very rough and full of large stones. It is always wet under foot and usually a little overgrown with gorse.

Carry on uphill between the boundary hedges and walls, where there is very little opportunity to see the surrounding countryside. The last stretch of the climb takes us on open land to the mountain gate. Now we can look behind and admire the view over Maughold and the patchwork of fields below us. Once through the gate the going, although still uphill, is less severe but well defined along a mountain track. Immediately above us and to our left is Slieau Ruy and the eastern flank of the northern hills.

The track skirts Slieau Ouyr and Slieau Lhean with Clagh Ouyr at first straight ahead of us. From this position we can see quite clearly the route

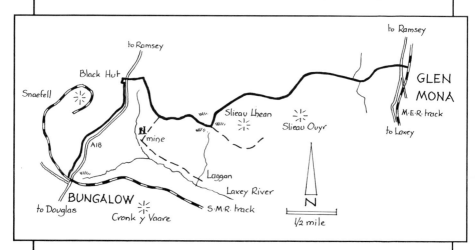

of our fourth walk, which is along the Barrule Ridge on our right. With North Barrule almost behind us we continue along the track.

The view changes as we swing round towards the saddle between Slieau Lhean and the tail of Clagh Ouyr. The valley to our right which we are now leaving is another of the Island's wild valleys — Cornah Valley.

The saddle we are crossing is on the route that miners followed to go to the North Laxey Mine, situated at the head of the valley below us.

We have to be careful here because we are approaching a junction between three paths and they meet in a bog just to make it more interesting! There is usually a signpost here (sometimes it blows down) and we want to turn right, picking our way through the bog to join the track ahead of us.

Now we are overlooking the Laxey Valley — the location of our first walk. To the left is Cronk y Vaare with the Snaefell Mountain Railway climbing its way to the Bungalow. This time we are looking down on it instead of up as we did on walk No 1.

You can see the route we took on that walk from the Bungalow down the side of the gully. Now you can see the true size of the gully bearing in mind that it starts from that little bog where we started the walk. It wasn't the little stream that carved the gully — its origins lie centuries earlier in the Ice Age when the ice sheet that covered the Island was melting and retreating.

We can't yet see the bulk of Snaefell, but as we continue the track winds round a bluff and there it is. The tramway can be seen as it appears at the summit and the Mountain Road is spread below us. The track continues on to join the road at the Black Hut but is not so clear. You will soon be able to see the TT marshals' shelter at the Black Hut below us.

Can you see the stone wall on this side of the road and the right of way signpost at the corner of the wall? Aim for the signpost and then follow the wall to the Snaefell Mountain Road. Between us and the road is large bog. It is often easier to either walk on the wall or the other side of it for a short distance, but be sure to get back onto the left hand side of the wall where the stream runs through the bog or you will get into more difficulty before you reach the road.

Cross the road and look for the gate in the mountain fence, the Ramsey side of the TT marshals' shelter. Go through it and walk round the back of the car park on the mountain side of the fence. We are going back to the Bungalow but taking the more leisurely route on the mountain, which is less arduous than dodging the traffic on the road. There is quite a well defined track made over the years by TT spectators that is used during the rest of the year by sheep.

Do you recall the dyke like depression I mentioned in the first walk? Well, we shall have to cross it shortly after leaving the Black Hut and it is probably easier to do that beside the mountain fence. After that it is easy going following the fence until we reach a gully, which was the start of the stream we crossed in walk No1. It is fairly easy to cross, the best place is on the concrete ledge by the fence.

Looking up the gully, alongside which Walk No 1 runs. The tram track is visible on the left and Beinn y Phott, climbed in Walk No 2, is in the background. (Stan Basnett)

Just ahead of us is the Les Graham Memorial. It is a marshals' shelter built to the memory of a famous TT rider who was killed in a race crash at the bottom of Bray Hill in 1953 while riding an Italian Gilera. The shape of the shelter was designed to represent praying hands and it commands a spectacular view over the Laxey valley. The route cuts away a little from the fence now as it approaches the Bungalow. There is ample opportunity to look at the trams coming and going on the track on the right hand side of the valley.

Now we come to the fence which surrounds the Motor Cycle Museum. There are stepping stiles over it, enabling us to complete our journey to the tram station and our return to Laxey.

Even if you are not very interested in motorcycling I would recommend a visit to the museum. There is a wealth of history contained in it and just to look at the bikes will make you realise how much development has taken place over the years. It is a place frequented by visitors to the Island more than by locals, which is a shame because it portrays a very important part of our heritage.

4. Barrule Ridge

6 1/2 miles
4 hours

A tricky but rewarding climb, giving spectacular coastal views and ending with a ride down Snaefell — after refreshments.

We have to take the Manx Electric tram to Ramsey, but ask the conductor to let you off at Walpole Road. Follow the tram track down to where it crosses Queens Pier Road, turn left and follow it to its junction with Mayhill and turn left. We are on the TT Course and shall follow it a short distance to the Ramsey Hairpin. The Motorcycle Museum better informs you about the names of these famous corners. Walk on the footways even though they change sides.

At the Hairpin, you can see where its name came from, look for the right of way sign and the path which will take you up the right hand side of Elfin Glen. We climb for about half a mile before reaching the Mountain Road above the Gooseneck. On the last section of the path we can see ahead of us the outline of North Barrule where our real climb begins.

Turn right at the road and follow it uphill for about quarter of a mile until we reach a lay-by and a stile over the mountain fence. This will give us access to the mountain which is not public land but owned by the Island's Water Authority, who together with their grazing tenant have given a right to walk on this land. Please respect the country code as ever.

Strike off up the side of the hill on a heading of 180°, making for the

View back towards North Barrule from Clagh Ouyr. (Stan Basnett)

top. On this approach to the summit the last 150 metres are quite steep once we cross the dilapidated stone boundary wall. The going is difficult with a great deal of broken slate, which can be slippy. There are also holes between the stones and sometimes these are covered with grass. Be careful where you put your feet.

Once at the top the view is stunning and you can look back the way you have come with some satisfaction. Ramsey and the northern plain are laid out some 1,800ft below you. Jurby Church lies roughly north west and its white outline is a distinct landmark on the edge of the coast. In the centre of the plain you should be able to see the village of Andreas and the Bride Hills. The Point of Ayre and its lighthouse is almost due north of us.

Following the coastline back towards Ramsey you will clearly see the sandy nature of the northern plain. Looking east you will see the village of Maughold and possibly Maughold Head and yet another of the Island's lighthouses. Below is the upper Cornah Valley and Park Llewellin and across the valley the eastern hills that featured on Walk No 3.

The best view is without doubt along the Barrule ridge, which is where we are going to walk following what has now become a quite well defined footpath on a heading of 242°. The view opens up quite dramatically as we move off from the summit. Snaefell is almost directly ahead of us. The ridge opens out below and we can see practically all of the northern hills. After crossing the first boundary wall the going is fairly easy, Snaefell drops in and out of view as we tackle the undulations of the ridge.

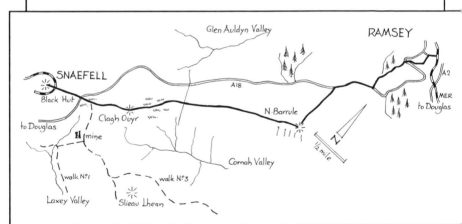

We are walking the boundary between two of the Island's seventeen parishes. On our right is the parish of Lezayre and on our left the parish of Maughold. The small piles of stone mark the boundary.

Now we are climbing the unnamed hill on the ridge, which is over 1,700ft and a pronounced summit, only to drop down yet again and cross another boundary wall to bring us back onto common land, still let for grazing.

Clagh Ouyr (1,808ft) is the last of the hills in the Barrule ridge and directly ahead of us — over a rather nasty bog. You can take a chance and go through the middle, but my advice is to head off to the right and pick your way past its westernmost edge on the watershed and then skirt round to the left, aiming for the bottom of the climb up to Clagh Ouyr. Pick up the path again and as you start the climb look back along the ridge, which will give you a spectacular view of an unusual aspect of North Barrule.

The climb up Clagh Ouyr is harder than it looks and when you get to what you think is the top you will find it has a number of false summits. At the top, you can see the Snaefell Mountain Railway climbing the side of Cronk y Vaare and then disappearing out of view as it climbs the western flank of Snaefell. It is immediately above you as it approaches the summit and where you no doubt had your appetite whetted for this walk when you were starting Walk No 2.

Now we make our way down to join the Mountain Road at the Black Hut. The route is easy to follow and is more or less straight down to the corner of the stone wall we followed on Walk No 3, avoiding yet another bog.

We cross the road and go through the gate. If you have had enough then you can take the route back to the Bungalow as described in Walk No 3, otherwise it is up to Snaefell's summit with me.

From the fence behind the marshals' shelter we head up on a bearing of 250°. If you haven't a compass then just head up keeping to the left of the rocky outcrops. There are good views to the right over Slieau Managh and towards Mount Karran and the Sulby Valley. In the foreground and below us can be seen Bloc Eary Reservoir.

The ground flattens a bit before starting to climb again and you might get a glimpse of the masts on the summit to check the direction. We should see the poles carrying the overhead for the trams. In any case we shall know when we are getting near because we start to encounter broken ground, similar to that near the top of North Barrule.

The summit is in sight now and we can go up to the top or walk beside the tram track to the Summit Hotel for refreshment and our return journey to Laxey.

Well, I trust that the weather for these walks has been the best that the Island can give and that you may be tempted to explore more.

COMING SOON

Fells Mountain Railways
by Keith Pearson

This book explores the lives of the inventor of the Fell system railway, John Barraclough Fell, and his son, George Noble Fell, and explains how the railway came to be used in Europe, South America and New Zealand.

Among the many topics covered are:-

➤ The origins of the Fell family from 1700.

➤ J B Fell's involvement with railway contracting and steamship operation in the southern Lake District — his 1845 *Lady of the Lake* was the first passenger steamer to be operated on an English lake.

➤ J B Fell's emigration to Italy and the extraordinary events of 1864-8, when Brassey, Fell and Company and their successor the Mont Cenis Railway Company constructed the 49-mile long Fell railway over the Mont Cenis pass, reaching an altitude of 6,827ft at its summit.

➤ Revealing correspondence from Thomas Brassey, Thomas Crampton and other major figures of the era.

➤ The Fells and the world of specialised patented narrow gauge railways.

➤ The South American Cantagallo Railway and the longer lived Rimutaka line in New Zealand (operated from 1878 to 1955).

➤ The genesis of the Snaefell Mountain Railway.

Appendices include the Fell patents and an "all time" listing of Fell locomotives. The book is illustrated with numerous drawings and maps, plans and photographs (including colour plates), many specially drawn for this work by Mr J C Cooke. The format resembles *100 years of the Manx Electric Railway (1993)*.

SPECIAL OFFER

Readers of this announcement are invited to become subscribers to "Fells Mountain Railways" at a special pre-publication price of £12 (names of subscribers will be listed in the usual manner). For an order form, please send a second class SAE to the author at Machell House, Brampton, Appleby in Westmorland, Cumbria CA16 6JS. Closing date December 31, 1995; publication planned for summer 1996.